HODDER GCSE HISTORY

THE REIGNS OF KING RICHARD I AND KING JOHN

1189–1216

Dale Banham

DYNAMIC LEARNING

HODDER
EDUCATION
LEARN MORE

Author's acknowledgement: I would like to thank Hadley Sharman and Caitlin Banham for their help with research and design features. I would also like to thank Ian Dawson and Ian Luff for their support with the writing of the book. Their creative ideas and constructive feedback were invaluable.

Acknowledgements

The Publishers would like to thank the following for permission to reproduce copyright material.

p.11 *Interpretations 3 and 4* © History Today.

For photo credits, see page 124.

Every effort has been made to trace all copyright holders, but if any have been inadvertently overlooked, the Publishers will be pleased to make the necessary arrangements at the first opportunity.

Note: The wording and sentence structure of some written sources have been adapted and simplified to make them accessible to all pupils while faithfully preserving the sense of the original.

Although every effort has been made to ensure that website addresses are correct at time of going to press, Hodder Education cannot be held responsible for the content of any website mentioned in this book. It is sometimes possible to find a relocated web page by typing in the address of the home page for a website in the URL window of your browser.

Hachette UK's policy is to use papers that are natural, renewable and recyclable products and made from wood grown in sustainable forests. The logging and manufacturing processes are expected to conform to the environmental regulations of the country of origin.

Orders: please contact Bookpoint Ltd, 130 Park Drive, Milton Park, Abingdon, Oxon OX14 4SE. Telephone: +44 (0)1235 827720. Fax: +44 (0)1235 400454. Email: education@bookpoint.co.uk. Lines are open from 9 a.m. to 5 p.m., Monday to Saturday, with a 24-hour message answering service. You can also order through our website: www.hoddereducation.co.uk

ISBN: 978 1 4718 6202 1

© Dale Banham 2016

First published in 2016 by
Hodder Education,
An Hachette UK Company
Carmelite House
50 Victoria Embankment
London EC4Y 0DZ

www.hoddereducation.co.uk

Impression number 10 9 8 7 6 5 4 3 2 1

Year   2020 2019 2018 2017 2016

Cover photos *left* © Anibaltrejo/iStock/Thinkstock; *right* King John Seated, 1250–59 (vellum), English School (13th century)/© British Library, London, UK/Bridgeman Images

Illustrations by Oxford Designers and Illustrators, Peter Lubach, Richard Duszczak and DC Graphic Design Limited

Typeset in ITC Legacy Serif Std Book 10/12pt by DC Graphic Design Limited, Hextable, Kent.

Printed in Italy

A catalogue record for this title is available from the British Library.

CONTENTS

1 Introducing King Richard I and King John

Richard I and his brother John are two of the most well-known and controversial monarchs in British history. Their reigns saw many dramatic events: family feuds, the Third Crusade, the loss of Normandy, rebellion, the granting of Magna Carta and a bloody civil war. This chapter outlines the key events and introduces you to the controversy that surrounds the reputations of Richard and John.

1.1 Introducing King Richard: The legendary hero

Richard I is famous as a legendary hero. After his death many legends were created about 'Richard the Lionheart'. He was remembered as the great soldier king who fought bravely against the odds on crusade to win back the Holy Land for the Christian Church. This was the king who was cruelly captured returning from crusade and who, on his release from prison, once again displayed his incredible military skills by winning back the lands that his evil brother, Prince John, and the cunning King of France had stolen from him.

Dramatic stories were produced to explain his nickname – the Lionheart. One told of how, while Richard was in captivity, the King of Germany, angry that his daughter had fallen in love with Richard, planned to murder him by having a hungry lion released into his cell. But Richard was able to kill the lion by thrusting an arm down the beast's throat and pulling out its heart – which he sprinkled with salt and ate in front of the king.

Even Richard's death formed part of the legend. According to one story, after being wounded in battle, Richard continued to fight, leading an assault with a crossbow bolt embedded in his head, and refusing to die until the castle his army was attacking was taken.

The model king

For many years after his death Richard was seen as a model of what a good king should be. In Victorian times, people looked back to the Middle Ages for heroes and inspiration. In 1851 there was a Great Exhibition in London. The Italian artist, Carlo Marochetti, was paid to make a larger-than-life statue of Richard to stand at the western entrance to the exhibition. The statue shows Richard portrayed as a national hero. After the exhibition the statue was moved to the Houses of Parliament, where it still stands today.

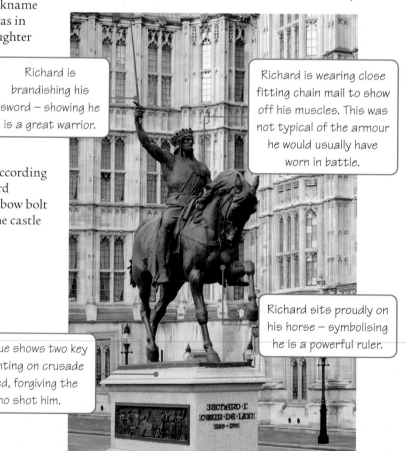

Richard is brandishing his sword – showing he is a great warrior.

Richard is wearing close fitting chain mail to show off his muscles. This was not typical of the armour he would usually have worn in battle.

Richard sits proudly on his horse – symbolising he is a powerful ruler.

The base of the statue shows two key events – Richard fighting on crusade and on his death bed, forgiving the crossbowman who shot him.

1.2 Introducing King John: The legendary villain

After Richard's death in 1199 his brother, John, became king. John's popular reputation is also linked to legend, especially the Robin Hood legend in which John is a cruel, greedy king who plots against his brother, puts innocent people in prison and raises unfair taxes.

In Walt Disney's 1973 cartoon film, John is shown as vain and cowardly; his crown constantly slips from his head because he has stolen it from Richard. In a more recent Hollywood film (2010), John is portrayed as a sly, cowardly, incompetent and completely dislikeable monarch. These films show how, in popular perception, John is 'Bad King John'.

How did people at the time view Richard and John?

Medieval **chroniclers** admired Richard. Roger of Wendover described Richard as 'the most victorious' and 'most wise' monarch. In contrast, chroniclers thought John was a failure. This can be seen in this picture of John, drawn by Matthew Paris, a monk from St Albans Abbey who lived from 1200 to 1259 and wrote a chronicle of English history from the Norman Conquest to the year 1253.

> Look at how John has been drawn – in particular his face and his pose. What message do you think Matthew Paris is trying to get across? **?**

> **HOW ARE RICHARD AND JOHN PORTRAYED TODAY?** **?**
>
> Find out more about Richard's and John's reputations by interviewing parents and relatives.
>
> 1. Ask the person you are interviewing to use three words to describe Richard and then three words to describe John.
> 2. Ask the person you are interviewing where their views come from:
>   - ☐ Their time at school
>   - ☐ Films and cartoons
>   - ☐ Legends and stories about Robin Hood
>   - ☐ History books.
> 3. Extra challenge: find other examples of how Richard and John have been portrayed in films, TV programmes, novels and legends.

Introducing the big question

How have historians interpreted Richard and John? Historical interpretations are not set in stone. Historians' views of Richard and John have changed over the years. The traditional, popular images of both kings have been challenged and debated.

The big question you will explore in this book is:

What reputation does each king deserve?

- Does Richard I deserve to be remembered as a success?
- Does John deserve his reputation as an incompetent failure?

In this book you will look at the evidence carefully and make up your own mind. To judge them properly you need to judge them by the standards of the time – this means developing a good understanding of the world in which they lived ... medieval society and the Angevin Empire.

> John's crown looks as if it is about to fall off his head. This gives the impression that John struggled to wear the crown properly and was not fit to be king. It also suggests that John was not in control of his kingdom.

> John is sitting on a campaign stool, not a throne. This implies that the country was never at peace and John was constantly fighting to win back land he had lost.

> John's body blocks out much of the church. This suggests John lacked respect for the Church. John was criticised by chroniclers for ignoring the rights of the Church and treating it badly.

1.3 Welcome to the family

Richard and John were born into a powerful family – the Angevins – who controlled land in England and overseas. However, it was far from a case of happy families. At times, their father, Henry II, struggled to control his unruly sons and powerful wife.

The father … Henry II (1154–89)

Henry was crowned King of England in 1154 but also ruled the vast Angevin Empire. Henry was a powerful figure on the European stage – King of England, Duke of Normandy, Count of Anjou and, through his marriage to Eleanor (the divorced wife of Louis VII of France), Duke of Aquitaine and Count of Poitou.

Henry has been described as 'a bully with brains and brawn'. He worked hard to establish law and order in England but his greatest challenge came from his own family. In 1173–74, encouraged by their mother, Henry's sons joined discontented barons and the King of Scotland to rebel against Henry. This revolt failed but more followed.

As you will see, the young Henry and Geoffrey rebelled again in 1183, and Richard rebelled in 1189. Henry died in 1189, ill and exhausted. During his last hours he heard that even his favourite son, John, had deserted him and joined Richard's rebellion.

The eldest son … Henry 'The Young King' (d.1183)

The young Henry was not prepared to wait for his father to die to have real power. He demanded that his father let him rule England, Normandy or Anjou on his own. In 1173, when his father refused to agree, the young Henry rebelled.

In 1182 the young Henry again asked his father for control of Normandy. By this point, Richard had Aquitaine, Geoffrey had Brittany but the young Henry seemed to have nothing. He rebelled again, joined by Geoffrey and Philip II, the new King of France. Richard fought alongside his father against his two brothers. The power struggle ended with the death from illness of the young Henry.

Richard (1189–99) m. Berengaria of Navarre

Richard was born in England in 1157 but spent most of his early life in Aquitaine and rarely saw his father. In 1172 Henry II decided to use his sons to help him rule his vast Empire. At the age of just fourteen, Richard became Duke of Aquitaine.

Richard joined his brothers in rebellion against Henry in 1173–74, but in 1182–83 he fought alongside his father against them. After the death of the young Henry, Richard became Henry II's heir. Henry II was now keen to provide for John – his favourite son – by giving him Aquitaine, but Richard refused to hand Aquitaine over to his brother.

In 1189, Richard rebelled again. He may have feared his father would disinherit him and name John as his heir. Richard was encouraged to rebel by Philip II and they joined forces in a successful attack on Henry's lands. Henry was forced to accept a humiliating peace treaty and died two days later. Richard was king.

THE ANGEVIN FAMILY TREE

?

Produce your own copy of the Angevin family tree. You will need to refer to this as you study the reigns of Richard and John in more detail. Keep your notes very brief. Try not to use more than ten words to record the key points about each of the key individuals in the family tree.

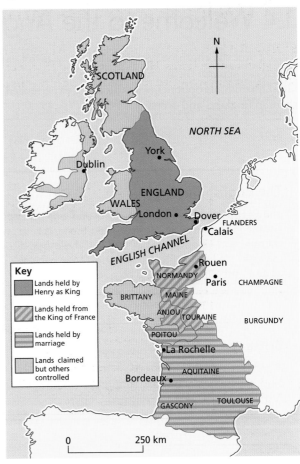

▲ A map of the Angevin Empire ruled over by Henry II.

Key
- Lands held by Henry as King
- Lands held from the King of France
- Lands held by marriage
- Lands claimed but others controlled

0   250 km

The mother … Eleanor of Aquitaine (d.1204)

Eleanor had been married to King Louis VII of France, but this marriage ended in 1152 and, aged 30, she married 19 year-old Henry II. Eleanor had inherited the Duchy of Aquitaine, a large area (one third of modern France) with great wealth and prestige.

Eleanor was powerful and ambitious. She seems to have channelled her own ambitions through her sons, encouraging them to rebel against Henry. From 1173, Henry kept her under armed guard – referring to her as his 'hated Queen'. After Henry died, Eleanor provided advice for Richard and John and helped them control their lands in France.

Geoffrey (d.1186) m. Constance of Brittany

Geoffrey joined his brother, the young Henry, in rebellion against his father in 1173–74. In 1181, Geoffrey became Duke of Brittany but this did not stop him rebelling against his father again in 1182–83. Geoffrey was known to attack monasteries and churches in order to raise money for his military campaigns. He was good friends with Philip II and spent a lot of time at the French court. Geoffrey was trampled to death in an accident at a jousting tournament in 1186. It was recorded by one chronicler that, at Geoffrey's funeral, the grief-stricken Philip attempted to jump into the coffin.

Arthur (d.1204)

As the son of Geoffrey, Arthur felt that he had a better claim to the throne than John. When Richard died, the twelve-year-old Arthur joined forces with Philip II and attacked John's lands in France.

John (1199–1216) m. Isabella of Angouleme

As Henry's youngest son, John was not expected to become king. In 1185 Henry sent John to extend control over Ireland. The expedition was a failure and John was called home after six months.

John first plotted with Richard against his father, and then against Richard when he went on crusade. When Richard returned, John threw himself at Richard's feet and begged for mercy. Richard forgave him and eventually named John as his heir. John became king in 1199.

1.4 Welcome to the Angevin Empire

Ruling over the enormous Angevin Empire was not easy. Some parts of the country needed a close eye kept on them, and kings could only travel on horseback. Richard and John also faced formidable opponents – skilled and experienced leaders who caused problems for them in England and overseas.

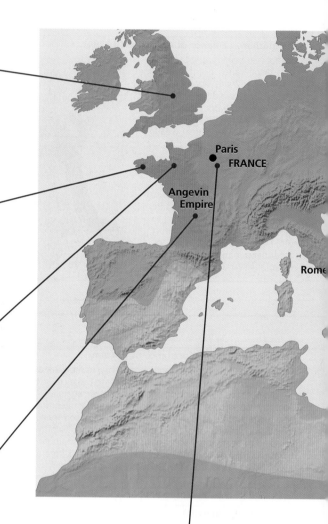

The English Barons

The barons were the most powerful and wealthy group of people in the country. They supplied the king with an army in wartime and helped him maintain law and order. If the king angered the barons they could rebel. They had their own castles and armies, so could be a real threat.

Brittany

Ruled by Geoffrey until his death in 1186. After Richard died, the barons of Brittany supported Geoffrey's son, Arthur, in his claim to the Angevin Empire.

Normandy

Closely linked with England since William of Normandy's invasion in 1066. Many wealthy families held land in both England and Normandy. Richard and John would need to defend Normandy to keep these wealthy barons onside.

The Duchy of Aquitaine

A region of great wealth and powerful barons.
There were frequent revolts by leading barons in Aquitaine.

Philip II, King of France

The land ruled by the King of France was smaller than modern-day France. However, Philip II was determined to weaken the Angevin Empire and extend his own lands. He was a skilled diplomat and a very good military tactician. 'Cunning' may be the best word to describe Philip! He was very good at taking advantage of his enemies' weaknesses.

Visible learning

Using a hypothesis to keep you focused (on the question)

A hypothesis is your first thoughts on the answer to a question. Having a hypothesis in your mind establishes a clear line of argument, although you may well change your mind later on. It helps you to keep the question in mind throughout the enquiry and stops you getting lost in too much information.

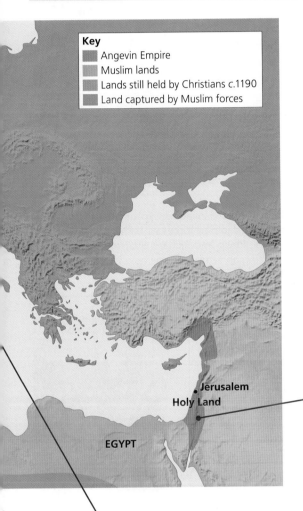

Key

- Angevin Empire
- Muslim lands
- Lands still held by Christians c.1190
- Land captured by Muslim forces

Jerusalem
Holy Land

EGYPT

CONSTRUCTING A HYPOTHESIS

1   It is time to make a prediction. We call this a hypothesis. Use the information on these two pages and the bullets below to construct a hypothesis in answer to the question: What is going to be Richard's and John's biggest challenge?
    - ☐ Dealing with troublesome barons in England.
    - ☐ Attacks from the King of France.
    - ☐ Challenges set by the Pope.
    - ☐ Family problems.

    Explain your answer. Then read pages 8–9 to see if you are right.

2   As you read the story on pages 8–9 make a note of questions you want to ask. You might want to ask questions about the causes of events (Why did …?) or the consequences (How did this affect …?). Some questions you might want to ask have been added in thought bubbles for the first two events on page 8. You may be able to replace them with more interesting ones.

3   When you have finished reading the story on pages 8–9 return to your hypothesis. How far was your prediction right? What was the biggest challenge to Richard and John? Explain your answer.

Saladin

A Christian army had captured the holy city of Jerusalem in 1099 during the First Crusade. The crusades were wars between Christian and Muslim armies in the area around Jerusalem (called the Holy Land). Some crusaders stayed in the Holy Land, gaining more territory from the Muslims who lived in the Middle East. In the second half of the twelfth century the Muslims began to fight back. Their leader, Saladin, created a large, well equipped and well trained army. He was able to reconquer large areas of the crusader kingdom. In 1187 he regained control of Jerusalem. The attempt by a Christian army to win back this land became known as the Third Crusade.

The Roman Catholic Church

All churches and monasteries in England were part of the Roman Catholic Church. The overall head of the Church was the Pope. This made him tremendously powerful. Popes often got involved in disputes in Europe. They also encouraged all Christians to defend the Holy Land in the Middle East as their main duty. Pope Gregory VIII called for a crusade to recapture Jerusalem from Saladin in 1187. Innocent III (pictured) became Pope when Gregory died in 1198. He was determined to have a say in what happened in the countries of western Europe.

1.5 The big story: An overview of the reigns of Richard and John, 1189–1216

How did Richard treat John? Did he give John any lands or responsibility?

1 Richard becomes king

Richard was greeted enthusiastically when he arrived in England in 1189. He was crowned king in September at Westminster Abbey in London. Richard had been fighting against his father, but he pardoned those men who had fought alongside Henry II against him. In 1190 Richard left England to tour his lands in France.

Did people support the crusade? Who did Richard leave in control of England?

2 The great English sell off

In 1187, Richard had agreed to go on a crusade to the Holy Land. Muslim forces, led by Saladin, had captured Jerusalem and the Pope had called for Christians to fight to bring it back. In order to pay for the crusade, Richard raised taxes and sold off everything he could offer – land, offices, earldoms and positions as sheriff.

3 A crusading hero

Richard set off on crusade to the Holy Land in June 1190 and invaded Cyprus on his way. He arrived in the Holy Land in June 1191. In July, Richard joined forces with Philip II's French army to capture the important port of Acre. However, Philip and Richard quarrelled and the French King returned home in August. Despite leading an army that was now weakened, Richard managed to defeat Saladin at the Battle of Arsuf in September.

4 Failure to take Jerusalem

The main aim of the Third Crusade had been to recapture Jerusalem. Richard attempted to take Jerusalem twice, but despite getting close to the Holy City the crusaders failed. Richard agreed a truce with Saladin. Jerusalem remained under Saladin's control but Christians would be allowed to visit the city. The crusaders also kept the ports they had fought so hard for – Jaffa and Acre – as well as the land in between.

5 Richard is captured

Richard left the Holy Land in October 1192. He travelled through Europe in disguise, hoping to avoid his enemies, but he was recognised in Vienna and imprisoned by the Duke of Austria. He was not released until February 1194, after a huge ransom had been paid. During this time his brother John and Philip II plotted to take control of his lands in England and France. By 1194 Philip had invaded large areas of Richard's lands in France.

6 Richard wins back his lands in France

Most of England had remained loyal to Richard and, on his return, John was forced to beg for his brother's forgiveness. By 1189 Richard had won back nearly all his land on the Continent. To defend Normandy and keep Philip under control, Richard built a huge fortress called Château Gaillard on the border between his and Philip's lands. In 1199, Richard was fatally wounded fighting in France. He named John as his heir.

7 John becomes king and Arthur disappears!

John's 12-year-old nephew, Arthur of Brittany, claimed that he should be king. Arthur joined with Philip and attacked John's lands. In 1202 John captured Arthur and put him in prison. Arthur was never seen again. One source claimed that John had killed Arthur in a drunken rage and then thrown his body in the River Seine.

8 Loss of Normandy

In 1200, John divorced his wife (Isabella of Gloucester) and married Isabella of Angouleme. Isabella had been promised to Hugh of Lusignan (a powerful French baron). Hugh complained to the King of France that John had not given him any compensation and Philip used this as an excuse to attack John's lands on the Continent. By 1204, John had lost Normandy and most of his other land on the Continent. Theses defeats earned John the nickname 'Soft-sword'.

9 Quarrel with the Pope

In 1205, John began a quarrel with the Pope over who should be the next Archbishop of Canterbury. John refused to accept Stephen Langton, the Pope's choice. In 1208, the Pope punished John by passing an **Interdict** over England and Wales. This meant that church services stopped and no marriages or burials could take place. John retaliated by seizing Church property. In 1209 the Pope **excommunicated** John. This meant that he would go to hell when he died. The quarrel ended in 1213 when John accepted Langton as Archbishop.

10 Quarrel with the barons

John was determined to regain the land that he had lost to Philip. He raised money to build a strong army by increasing taxes and introducing harsh fines (amercements) on his barons. Many got into debt and found themselves or their family locked up in prison. Some died horrible deaths. To make matters worse, the army that John raised was defeated in France. At the Battle of Bouvines, Philip was almost killed when he was knocked from his horse, but he was rescued and went on to win what was a lengthy and bloody battle.

11 Magna Carta

John's defeat in France was the final straw for many barons. By 1214 many were starting to think that John needed to change the way he ruled the country. When John refused to listen to their demands, they rebelled. In 1215 the rebel barons captured London and, in June, they forced John to agree to a set of rules about how to govern the country. This set of rules became known as Magna Carta, one of the most famous documents in history.

12 Civil war and a French invasion

John did not change his ways after signing Magna Carta and even asked the Pope to declare the document invalid. The barons invited Prince Louis (the son of the King of France) to take over as king. This led to a brutal civil war, as John and his supporters found themselves fighting against the rebel barons and a large French army. John died in October 1216, but the war continued. Eventually, after major battles at Lincoln and off the coast of Sandwich in 1217, Louis was defeated.

1.6 The big question: How far do Richard and John deserve their reputations?

How have views of Richard changed?

On pages 2–3 you were introduced to the traditional view of Richard and John – the great military hero who was replaced by his cruel and incompetent brother. This was very much the way that people writing at the time presented Richard and John. You have already seen how Matthew Paris portrayed John (see page 3 and below). Look at how he represented Richard I in the picture to the right on this page and compare it to his drawing of John. What differences can you see? What clues in the picture show that Matthew Paris respected Richard?

Matthew Paris' picture sums up how medieval chroniclers saw Richard – powerful and majestic, someone to be admired. Even writers from different backgrounds praised him. Ibn al-Athir, a Muslim historian from the thirteenth century wrote:

> Richard's courage, shrewdness, energy and patience made him the most remarkable ruler of his times.

A mainly positive image of Richard continued through to the Victorian period. Richard came to represent the English nation – a man whose wars were a demonstration of superiority over other nations – especially the French. For example, in the seventeenth century, historian John Speed saw Richard as 'a noble prince' whose rule 'showed his love and care of the English nation'. The Victorian view of Richard is best symbolised by the huge statue that stands outside of the Houses of Parliament (see page 2).

INTERPRETATIONS OF RICHARD ?

Look back at the overview of the reign of Richard on page 8.

1 What evidence can you find to support the five criticisms of Richard in bold in box 1 on page 11?

2 What evidence can you find to support the five positive views of Richard in bold in box 2 on page 11?

How have views of John changed?

According to John's contemporaries, such as Roger of Wendover, John was a complete failure and an evil ruler. A few years later, Matthew Paris summed up John's reign:

> John was a tyrant rather than a king, a destroyer rather than a governor, an oppressor of his own people … Foul as it is, hell itself is made fouler by the presence of King John.

In contrast, Tudor historians at the time of Henry VIII (1509–47) admired John. They thought the barons were wrong to rebel against him and that John was right to stand up to the Pope (just as Henry had done).

Victorian historians, like the medieval chroniclers, saw him as a cruel and wicked king. Kate Northgate, writing in 1902, accused John of cowardice, weakness, sloth and superhuman wickedness. But what about recent historians? Since the 1950s there has been a debate about the kind of reputation John deserves.

INTERPRETATIONS OF JOHN ?

Look back at the overview of John's reign on page 9.

1 What evidence can you find to support the three positive views of John in bold in box 1 on page 11?

2 What evidence can you find to support the three criticisms of John in bold in box 2 on page 11?

The big debate: Critics of Richard I versus his defenders

1 CRITICISMS OF RICHARD I

Over time, some historians began to criticise Richard.

The eighteenth century historian, Laurence Echard, labelled Richard 'the king who was never there'. Richard was criticised as **a king who neglected his kingdom** and wasted its resources abroad.

In the twentieth century, some historians continued to follow this line of argument. They criticised Richard's government of England. Austin Lane Poole criticised Richard for his **lack of political wisdom**. Poole suggests that Richard made bad decisions when ruling the country.

Michael Markowski, called Richard **'a dismal failure'**. He argued that Richard should not be seen as a hero but instead a king **obsessed with war**: 'a man who merely wanted to fight hand to hand forever'.

French historians have argued that his **actions on crusade were brutal and stupid**.

2 THE CASE FOR THE DEFENCE

In the last twenty years, some modern historians have seen Richard in a far more positive light. They argue that Richard was a very skilful military leader who **successfully defended the Angevin Empire**.

Thomas Asbridge argues that Richard was **a military genius**: 'the best commander of his generation' and 'a fearsome opponent, unrivalled among the crowned monarchs of Europe'.

Historians such as John Gillingham, have argued that as well as being a great military leader, Richard was a skilled diplomat and **a clever politician**. They argue that Richard was not an irresponsible monarch who neglected England. Instead they present him as a king who **set up a strong system of government** that did not always need the king to be there, personally making decisions.

In addition, they praise Richard for the way he **kept his barons 'onside'** and developed a good relationship with the Church.

The big debate: Defenders of John versus his critics

1 THE CASE FOR THE DEFENCE

Since the 1950s some historians have challenged the negative view of John. They argue that John was **an intelligent, hard-working king** who did a great deal to improve the royal government: an 'administrative genius'.

W.L. Warren, in the 1960s, highlighted the size of the problems John faced. This led to some historians presenting John as **an unlucky king** who faced an impossible task to keep the Angevin Empire together. He lacked the resources he needed and faced an experienced and dangerous opponent.

David Bates (writing in 1994) argued that: 'In some areas John faced impossible difficulties. In others he was **close to success**. John's failure deserves some sympathy.'

2 CRITICISMS OF JOHN

However, many modern historians see John as a failure. They accept he did face significant problems, but argue that John created many of these problems for himself.

For John Gillingham (writing in 1984) 'John was a very poor king. He was **useless at his most important job, managing the barons**.'

As a soldier, John was given the name 'Soft-sword' by contemporaries and many modern historians have argued that this reputation was deserved. Marc Morris argues that John was a **'poor soldier'**:

> John lacked boldness ... He relished the prospect of conflict, so long as the odds were stacked entirely in his favour ... As soon as the outcome seemed anything less than certain ... the king preferred to cut and run.

Historians have also argued that John's reputation for cruelty was fully deserved. David Carpenter says that the sources indicate that John was 'a fractured personality, suspicious, untrustworthy, **aggressive and cruel**'.

2 Life in England 1189–1216

You need to be careful not to judge Richard and John by modern-day standards. To judge Richard and John fairly you need to reach judgements based on the standards of the time. This means building up a good understanding of medieval society.

- Chapter 2 will help you build a good knowledge and understanding of English society at the time and potential threats to the king's position.
- Chapter 3 will explore the main duties and responsibilities of a medieval monarch before going on to explore how Richard and John secured power and governed the country.

2.1 English society in 1189: The feudal hierarchy

England's population in 1189 was around 3.5 million. Wealth and power was not shared out equally among the population. There was a very rigid **feudal hierarchy**. The ladder on page 13 shows the different groups within society and their place in the feudal hierarchy. The higher up the ladder you were, the more wealth, power and freedom you had. It was very hard to move up the ladder and become wealthier and more powerful. If you were born a **peasant** it was highly likely that you would spend your whole life as a peasant. Each group had its own price, known as a 'wergild' (which translates as 'man-price'). If you killed a lord (a noble or a knight), you paid his family 1,200 shillings. If you killed a villein, you paid 200.

EXPLAINING LINKS BETWEEN DIFFERENT TYPES OF PEOPLE

Use an A3 piece of paper or a double page in your book to explain the links shown in the concept map below.

- Step 1: Start by using page 13 to explain the links labelled with a question mark.
- Step 2: Then use pages 14–16 to add extra detail to your diagram. Aim to add additional links that explain how different types of people were connected.

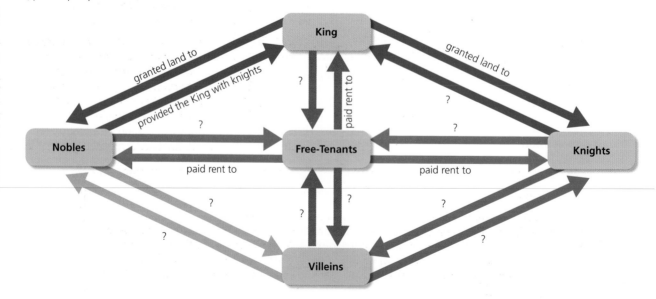

The feudal hierarchy

King

At the top of medieval society was the king. Richard and John were far more powerful than a modern-day monarch. A medieval monarch was tremendously rich and powerful. He owned huge areas of England and could reward his followers with positions of power. Kings decided how the country would be governed and made all the key decisions. The king's income per year depended on the taxes he raised, but it averaged around £22,000.

Nobles

Nobles varied greatly in wealth and the amount of land they held. Nobles would never do any physical work on the land. In 1066, William the Conqueror had won control of England with the help of his nobles and knights from Normandy. The first thing William did was give roughly 50 per cent of the land to the 150 leading nobles who had fought for him. In return they had to promise to help him rule the country and supply an agreed number of knights to fight for him. These leading nobles were known as tenants-in-chief or, more commonly, as barons. These barons were closest to the king in terms of rank and status. To use a modern term – they were the 'A list' nobles. They owned the land for life. The average income for a baron was £200 per year.

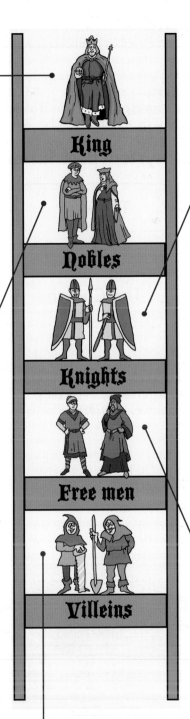

Knights

Usually knights were the younger sons of nobles who had not inherited their family title. They were sent to other noble families to train as knights. The title 'knight' was awarded only to those with noble blood in their veins who had shown themselves to be worthy of the title. It had to be earned by showing military skill and prowess. There were about 4,500 knights in the country, varying greatly in wealth and power. A few hundred of these were granted land by the king. The majority would have been given land by the barons. Knights played an important role in local communities and served on juries in the counties. The king employed knights in a variety of roles in local government. For example, they were employed as sheriffs, coroners and forest officials.

Free men

A free man could be a merchant, a professional soldier, a craftsman or a farmer who was a free tenant. Free men were free to travel and work for whomever they chose. Merchants tended to live in the towns. A well-off merchant would earn around £20 per year.

Free men who lived in the countryside were known as free tenants. They paid rent to the lord to farm their land. Many held between 30 and 100 acres of land from the local lord. Both free tenants and merchants served on juries.

Villeins

It is estimated that half of England's population were unfree peasants (also called villeins). They worked on their lord's land or for a free tenant. In return for this they were allowed to work a tiny piece of land for themselves, living off the crops they produced. They had no rights whatsoever and even had to ask permission for their daughters to marry. Villeins could not leave their manor (village) without permission and they could be bought and sold by their lord.

2.2 The nature of feudalism

English society in 1189 was organised around a set of relationships known as the feudal system. The feudal system centred on landholding. All land in England belonged to the king, and everyone from the richest to the poorest held his land from the king, either directly as a tenant-in-chief or indirectly as a tenant of one of the king's tenants-in-chief. In return for land, tenants made important promises to the king or their tenant-in-chief. Land would revert to the lord if the tenant was convicted of any crime. This was known as forfeiture. Tenants would forfeit their right to land if the king thought they were guilty of any wrong doing.

The feudal system part 1: How was land distributed?

The king

The lords

About 50 per cent of the land went to the barons – the leading nobles in the country. These barons would have owned hundreds of manors (a manor was land centred around one or more villages). Roger Bigod owned 6 in Essex, 117 in Suffolk and 187 in Norfolk. Knights and lesser nobles owned about 5 per cent of the land and considerably fewer manors (sometimes only one or two each). All nobles and knights holding land were known as lords.

The Church

The Church owned approximately 25 per cent of the land. As we will see later in this chapter, religion was an important part of medieval life and kings were keen to keep the Pope happy and to show respect for God. Church lands were expected to provide knights for the king. To provide money to pay for these the Church also rented its land to free men or lesser nobles.

The royal demesne

The king kept about 20 per cent of the land. This land was known as the royal demesne. Paid managers ran this land on the king's behalf and rented much of it out to free men. This gave the king a regular income with which to pay soldiers if he needed to. Some of the royal demesne was kept for royal hunting.

Visible learning

Using analogies to help you remember key features

To help you remember how land was divided up in England – think of the country as a football pitch.

The barons owned roughly one entire half – in return for loyalty and supplying knights to fight

The lesser nobles and knights had half of the centre circle

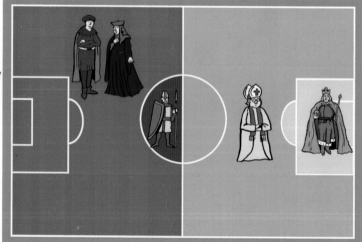

The king kept roughly one penalty area as 'the royal demesne'

The Church roughly had the rest of the other half of the pitch

The feudal system part 2: What was given in return for land?

Barons held their land directly from the king. The land held by a baron as a tenant-in-chief from the king was called a fief or fee. In return for this land they had to make important promises.

1 HOMAGE

The act of **homage** came at the start of the relationship between the king and a tenant-in-chief. When a new tenant succeeded to land they would kneel down, place their hands between the hands of the king and declare loyalty in return for the land. It created a bond between the king and his tenant-in-chief.

2 MILITARY SERVICE

The tenant-in-chief provided knights when a king raised an army. Some barons were allowed to pay money to the king instead of providing knights. This was known as '**scutage**' or shield money. Scutage was paid at a fixed rate according to the number of fiefs held by the tenant-in-chief. The more land you held, the more you paid.

What happened when a baron died?

When a baron died their land could only be passed on by royal approval. This was usually given in return for homage and a considerable sum of money. A new tenant-in-chief was expected to pay the king a relief when they inherited or gained an estate.

The king also had the rights of wardship over an heir who was under age. These rights meant that the king held the lands of the heir until they came of age. Alternatively, he could give or sell these rights to someone else.

Managing the barons

Barons could gain a great deal from showing loyalty to their king, but this did not make managing them easy. As you will see, many kings had problems controlling the barons.

It was believed that kings were chosen by God to protect and govern their people. Everyone had a duty to obey the king. However, it was also believed that kings had to govern well and some barons believed that they had the right to rebel if the king did not govern fairly.

Managing the barons was a balancing act.

On the one hand, a successful King had to keep the barons under control and make sure they did not become too powerful.

On the other hand, it was important to keep the barons 'onside' and make them feel involved in running the country. They were rich and powerful. They had their own armies and their own castles. The King needed their support at times of war.

ADDING TO YOUR CONCEPT MAP

Use the information on pages 14–15 to add extra details to your concept map from page 12 showing the relationship between the king and his barons. Make sure you use the following key terms:

- homage
- scutage
- a fief
- rights of wardship
- a relief
- forfeiture.

COMPLETING YOUR CONCEPT MAP ?

1 Use the information boxes below to complete your concept map from page 12 showing the links between the different types of people in feudal society. Make sure you add and explain links between:
  □ barons and knights
  □ the lords (barons and knights) and those whom they granted land to (free tenants and villeins) .

2 Design an analogy or draw a cartoon that explains:
  □ knight service
  □ land service.

KEY FEATURE 1: KNIGHT SERVICE

A key feature of the feudal system was **knight service**. Under the feudal system, the relationship a knight had with his baronial lord mirrored that between the king and his barons. In return for land the knights provided military service. Barons granted sections of their land to lesser nobles and knights in return for homage and military service.

The knight had to do homage to his lord (usually a baron but sometimes the king) for the land that he held from him. The lord also expected money payments in the form of a relief when the knight inherited land. When a knight died, his lord had rights of wardship over his estate until his heir came of age. Knights would also be expected to contribute to the payment of any ransom demanded if their lord was captured and imprisoned.

KEY FEATURE 2: LABOUR SERVICE

Nobles and knights would often rent land to free men who farmed it and paid a sum of money for doing so. Free men also had to help the lord at harvest time and with ploughing. This was known as **labour service**. A free man had to pay the lord to use his mill to grind his corn into flour. They could not even bake their own bread – they had to use the lord's ovens or pay his bakers. Sons of free men had to pay the lord a sum of money to take over their father's lands.

Working on the land of all lords and free men were the unfree labourers known as villeins. Villeins also had to perform labour service. They worked for the lord throughout the year, doing jobs such as ploughing, weeding and mending fences. In return for this they were given a small piece of land, on which they could grow their own crops.

Practice question

Describing the key features of a period

Use the advice below to answer the following practice questions:
1 Describe two features of knight service between 1189 and 1216.
2 Describe two features of labour service between 1189 and 1216.

For 'describe' questions you need to do more than simply list points. Look at the example below – you need to develop the points you make – aim to support your 'big points' about life in medieval England with 'little points' that **describe the key features** of life in 1189.

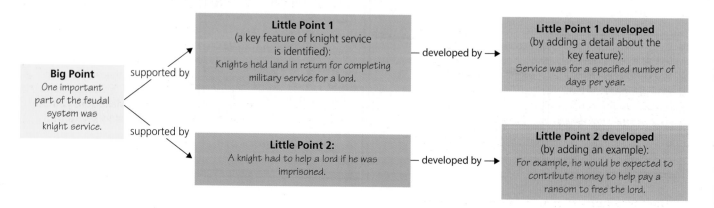

Big Point
One important part of the feudal system was knight service.

— supported by →

Little Point 1
(a key feature of knight service is identified):
Knights held land in return for completing military service for a lord.

— developed by →

Little Point 1 developed
(by adding a detail about the key feature):
Service was for a specified number of days per year.

— supported by →

Little Point 2:
A knight had to help a lord if he was imprisoned.

— developed by →

Little Point 2 developed
(by adding an example):
For example, he would be expected to contribute money to help pay a ransom to free the lord.

2.3 What was life like in the countryside?

Nearly everyone in the Middle Ages lived in villages in the countryside. These villages, with land around them, were called manors. The land was held and controlled by the lord of the manor (usually a baron, but sometimes a knight). Most people spent their time working hard on the land and rarely left their village. News travelled slowly. For most peasants the lord of the manor was more important than the king.

What does the evidence reveal about the nature of agricultural life?

In order to find out about life in the countryside we are going to explore two types of evidence:

- An artist's reconstruction of what a typical medieval village looked like (see pages 18–19). The village, Wharram Percy, no longer exists but the reconstruction is based on archaeological evidence.
- The Luttrell Psalter. These illustrations were part of a manuscript that was paid for by Sir Geoffrey Luttrell to show life in the manor of Irnham in Lincolnshire. The Psalter was produced in the first half of the fourteenth century. Agricultural life in the early thirteenth century would have been very similar to this and the detailed illustrations give us a good insight into peasant life in particular.

The Luttrell Psalter

▲ A Ploughing – land was ploughed before seed was planted. The plough was pulled by oxen.

▲ B Clod-breaking – to stop the plough getting stuck, clumps of soil had to be broken up with large mallets.

▲ C Sowing – The seed was scattered by hand.

▲ D Harvest time – harvesting was done by men, women and children. The corn was cut with a scythe and then taken away in bundles. Children picked up every little piece so nothing was wasted.

▲ E Spinning – the wool from sheep was spun into thread and then used to make clothes or blankets.

LIFE IN THE COUNTRYSIDE: PART 1

Use the information on pages 18–19 to work out the time of year when activities A–D from the Luttrell Psalter would have taken place.

A moment in time: Life in Wharram Percy c.1200

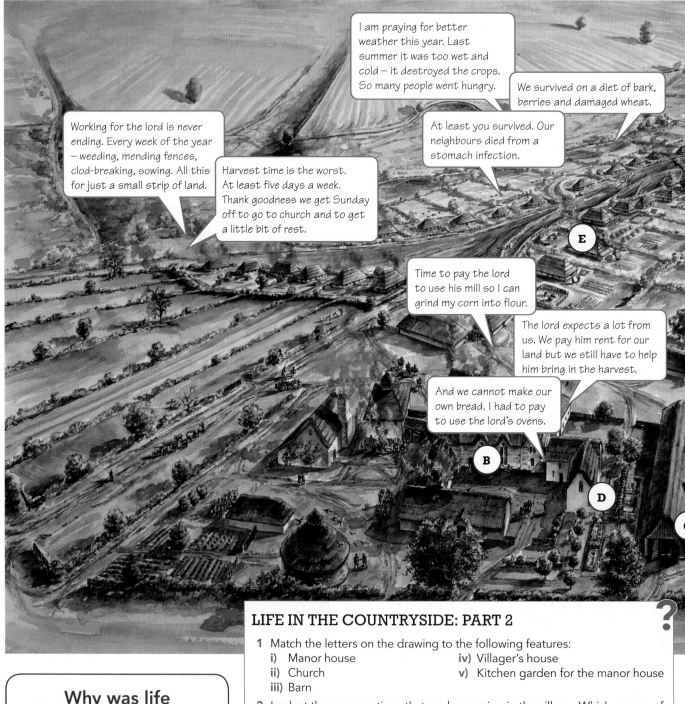

I am praying for better weather this year. Last summer it was too wet and cold – it destroyed the crops. So many people went hungry.

We survived on a diet of bark, berries and damaged wheat.

Working for the lord is never ending. Every week of the year – weeding, mending fences, clod-breaking, sowing. All this for just a small strip of land.

At least you survived. Our neighbours died from a stomach infection.

Harvest time is the worst. At least five days a week. Thank goodness we get Sunday off to go to church and to get a little bit of rest.

Time to pay the lord to use his mill so I can grind my corn into flour.

The lord expects a lot from us. We pay him rent for our land but we still have to help him bring in the harvest.

And we cannot make our own bread. I had to pay to use the lord's ovens.

Why was life expectancy low?

It is estimated that 20–30 per cent of children died before the age of seven – they were particularly vulnerable to starvation and diseases such as smallpox, whooping cough, measles, tuberculosis, influenza and stomach infections.

LIFE IN THE COUNTRYSIDE: PART 2

1 Match the letters on the drawing to the following features:
   i) Manor house
   ii) Church
   iii) Barn
   iv) Villager's house
   v) Kitchen garden for the manor house

2 Look at the conversations that are happening in the village. Which groups of people would have been talking like this? Choose an option from the bullet points below. You may want to look back at page 13 to remind yourself of the different groups of people.
   ☐ A conversation between villeins
   ☐ A conversation between free men
   ☐ This conversation could have been had by villeins or free men.

3 Use the information on pages 17–19 and the writing advice on page 16 and page 115 at the end of the book to describe the key features of agricultural life. Make sure you describe at least two features.

January–February. Land is given out by the lord

May–July. Growing the crops

March. Preparing the land

August–September. Harvesting the crops

April–May. Sowing the seeds

October–November. Storing the crops

Why was the king important to people living in the countryside?

The way that a king governed affected the lives of everyone in the countryside – even the peasants. The king had responsibility to provide peace and stability. A king who failed to control the country could cause problems – civil war and rebellion often meant that lives were disrupted as crops could be destroyed and food taken to provide for soldiers. Wars and rebellions also brought violence, chaos and disorder to people's lives.

A king could cause hardship to free tenants by raising taxes. If the king expected more money from his barons and **sheriffs** they expected more money from the people who worked the land.

2.4 A moment in time: What was life like in the towns?

Although most people lived in villages there were some small towns. This is an artist's reconstruction of the town of Ludlow in the thirteenth century. It gives you an idea of what towns were like in the medieval period. As you will see, towns played an important role in the economy because they were the main centres of trade and held markets where goods could be bought and sold.

LIFE IN TOWNS

1 Use the information aound the image to describe the key features of life in towns. Remember to use the advice on pages 16 and 115 to help you write an effective description.

2 Compare life in towns to life in the countryside. Can you spot any similarities? Aim to identify and describe three similarities.

The economy was expanding and towns were growing in size. The wealth of towns was growing from trade and manufacture. England's main imports were wine and high-quality cloth that was imported from Flanders. The main export was wool.

Some people living in towns were merchants – they could become rich by selling food, clothes or luxuries at markets and fairs. Many people living in towns were poor and did very ordinary jobs such as working as servants or raking the streets clean of muck.

People from nearby villages would visit the town to buy and sell goods in the market. Local villagers would send their surplus goods such as eggs, cheese or vegetables. At the market the villagers would buy things that they could not make at home – such as shoes or cooking pots.

Towns were dirty places. Many people kept animals, just as they did in the countryside. There were no sewers so rubbish and excrement sometimes littered the streets. Life expectancy was low and diseases spread rapidly in cramped and dirty conditions.

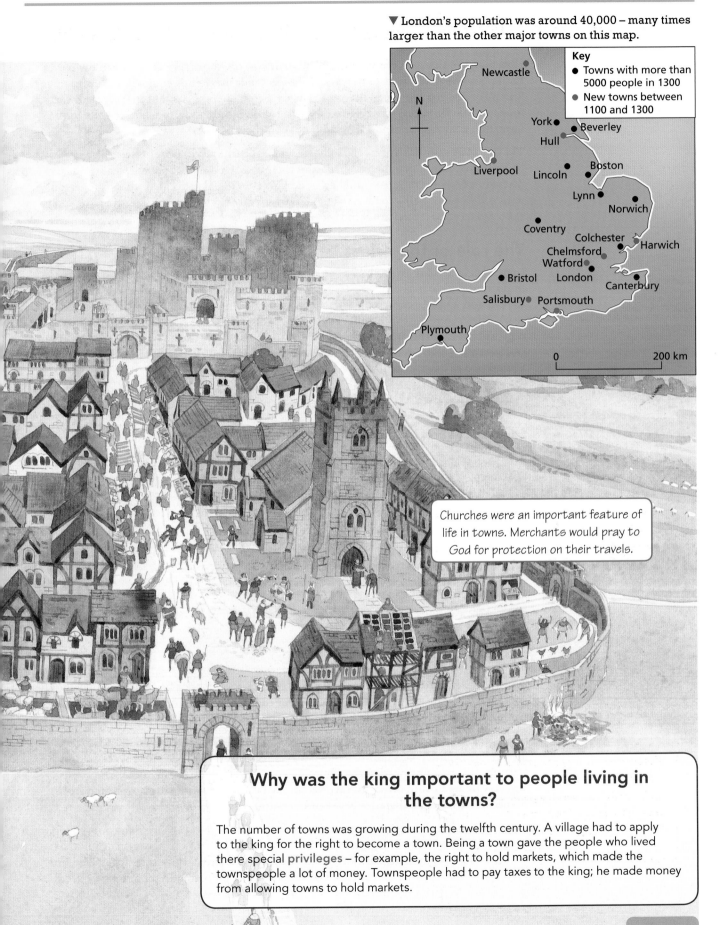

▼ London's population was around 40,000 – many times larger than the other major towns on this map.

Key
● Towns with more than 5000 people in 1300
● New towns between 1100 and 1300

Newcastle

York● ●Beverley
Hull●

Liverpool● Lincoln● ●Boston

Lynn● ●Norwich

Coventry●
Colchester●
Chelmsford● ●Harwich
Watford●
Bristol● London● ●Canterbury

Salisbury● ●Portsmouth

Plymouth●

0   200 km

Churches were an important feature of life in towns. Merchants would pray to God for protection on their travels.

Why was the king important to people living in the towns?

The number of towns was growing during the twelfth century. A village had to apply to the king for the right to become a town. Being a town gave the people who lived there special **privileges** – for example, the right to hold markets, which made the townspeople a lot of money. Townspeople had to pay taxes to the king; he made money from allowing towns to hold markets.

2.5 What was the role of the Church in people's lives?

How many similarities did you find between life in the countryside and life in towns? In both places disease was common and life expectancy was low. Inequality was also a major feature of life in towns and villages. In towns, rich merchants could earn large sums of money, while labourers struggled to survive. In the countryside, peasants faced a life of hardship, while barons and earls had land, wealth and power.

The one major similarity was the importance of the Church in people's lives. People believed that God controlled every part of their lives. God made them healthy or ill, and determined whether there would be a good harvest. God also decided whether a person went to heaven or hell – so pleasing God in your daily life was very important. Everyone was expected to go to church on Sundays and holy days.

The role of the priest

In nearly every village there was a church and a priest. The priest was one of the most important people in the village. He helped the poor and elderly and taught some children to read and write. In return the villagers paid him a tithe (a tenth of all their crops every year). Priests were meant to help people live good lives so that they would go to Heaven. It was believed that the most important thing to do to get to Heaven was to attend a church service, called mass, delivered by the priest every Sunday. Priests were not allowed to marry as they had to devote themselves to God.

?

THE IMPORTANCE OF RELIGION

1 Describe two features of the role of a priest. Use the guidance on pages 16 and 115 to help you write an effective description.

2 Explain why religion was so important to people living at the time. Make sure that you mention the following key terms in your explanation:
   ☐ God
   ☐ Church
   ☐ Heaven
   ☐ Hell
   ☐ Purgatory.

Monasteries

There were around 900 monasteries in England where monks held prayer services. They also looked after the poor and the sick.

The influence of the Church

The Church had a great deal of wealth and power. Some bishops had incomes that equalled those of the greatest barons. Over a quarter of the land in England was controlled by the Church. Much of this land was held directly from the king in return for the same services that were provided by the barons and earls.

The English Church was part of a much bigger religious organisation – the Roman Catholic Church. The head of the Church was the Pope who lived in Rome. The Pope was very powerful and often got involved in the politics of countries in western Europe. Sometimes this led to disputes between kings and the Pope.

The Pope could call for Christians to join a crusade against non-Christian countries to protect the Church or the Holy Land in Jerusalem. The Pope was a powerful ally and his support could help motivate troops going into battle, as they felt that they had God on their side. All of this meant that it was very important for medieval monarchs to build good relations with the Church.

How far did Christianity rule peoples' lives?

People believed that life after death was more important than their life on Earth and that Heaven, Hell and Purgatory were real places. They were desperate to keep out of Hell where they would remain in agony for eternity (for the rest of time). People believed that nearly everyone went to Purgatory when they died. How long anyone spent there depended on how sinful they had been and how much good they had done when they were alive. The more you pleased God through your actions, the less time you spent in Purgatory before going to Heaven. The box below shows the actions you could take to please God.

Heaven
Where those who have paid for their sins in Purgatory join God, Jesus Christ and the saints.

Purgatory
Where nearly everyone goes to be punished for their sins. The pains and torments are almost as bad as those in Hell but when people have paid for their sins they go to Heaven.

Hell
Where those whose sins are so terrible they cannot be forgiven go. The pains of Hell are far worse than any pain suffered on Earth.

HOW COULD YOU SPEND LESS TIME IN PURGATORY?

1. Go to church every week and pray for forgiveness.
2. Donate money to have prayers said for your soul. The richer you are the more prayers you can pay for. Some wealthy people were able to pay for a special chapel to be built where priests could be employed to say prayers for their soul.
3. Help improve the lives of the poor – by giving them food, money or clothes.
4. Go on a pilgrimage to Canterbury, Rome or Jerusalem. It was thought that the further you travelled, the more sins would be forgiven.
5. Go on a crusade to fight and reclaim Jerusalem – the most important holy city for all Christians (as it was the place where it was believed that Jesus was buried – in the church of the Holy Sepulchre – before he ascended to Heaven).

Look at the box on the left.

1. Which actions could only be chosen by the rich?
2. Which actions could be chosen by everyone?

Visible learning

Making connections

It is important to make connections between different parts of your GCSE course. The role and influence of the Church helps to explain peoples' attitudes and actions in later chapters.

THINK FORWARD AND CONNECT

The Crusades are a key part of Chapter 4. How does this section help to explain why men risked their lives on crusades?

2.6 What was the role of Jews in medieval England?

In the middle ages, Jews began to settle in towns around England. By 1189 there were about 5,000 Jews living in England's towns. Jews were an important feature of economic life and they were protected by the king. Why was this?

> I make a lot of profit from the business activities of Jews. When a Jew dies, all the people who owe me money still have to pay it back. The money they owe and all the interest has to be paid into my treasury. This brings me in a lot of money every year. I can also raise money by taxing the Jews. I do not have to ask permission for this.

Royal exploitation

As you can see, medieval kings could make a lot of money from Jews. The main way that Jews were exploited was through taxation. At any time, the king had the right to force Jews to pay special taxes (known as tallages).

Legal status

All the possessions owned by Jews were the king's property. However, Jews did benefit from certain privileges granted by the king. They had the right to travel freely and to buy and sell goods. They could move wherever they wanted and they could charge interest for lending money.

Role in moneylending

The Church banned Christians from lending money. If barons or knights needed money to buy or inherit land, they borrowed it from Jewish moneylenders. In return for lending money, people had to pay the moneylenders interest on the money they borrowed, which meant that they paid back a lot more than they borrowed. Interest rates could be as high as 40 per cent per year, which meant that if you borrowed £100 for a year you paid back £140. As a result, some Jews, like Aaron of Lincoln, became rich and powerful people within their local area. Some barons ran up large debts, borrowing money to buy the rights to land from the king and to buy important positions (**offices**) within the government.

THE ROLE OF JEWS ❓

Read the story on page 25. What could explain this vicious attack on the Jews of York in 1190? Use the information on this page, including the case study of Aaron of Lincoln, to help you.

AARON OF LINCOLN

- Born in Lincoln (about 1125).
- Believed to have been the wealthiest man in England.
- Had **agents** working for him who lent people money (and in return charged interest).
- Lent a lot of money to people who wanted to build abbeys and monasteries. The abbey at St Albans, Peterborough Cathedral and Lincoln Minster were all built with money lent by Aaron of Lincoln.
- Died in 1186 – the money that people owed Aaron now had to be paid to the king (Henry II).
- It is estimated that, at the time of his death, about 430 barons and knights owed Aaron of Lincoln a total of £15,000.
- Henry also took over everything that Aaron of Lincoln owned (this included land and money). The money was sent over to France to help Henry in his war against Philip II but the ship carrying the money sank.

Case study: York 1190

By the time that Richard I came to the throne the Jewish community in York was well established. York was the one city north of Lincoln where Jews settled in significant numbers.

The attacks on Jews living in York started in March. One stormy night, a band of armed men broke into the home of Benedict, a Jew who had recently died. The men killed all the Jews living in the house, including Benedict's widow and children. They set the roof on fire and stole any valuables they found. The next day 150 Jews asked for protection from the royal constable of York castle.

The constable agreed to protect them. After his coronation as king in 1189, Richard I had ordered that no Jews should be attacked and that they were under his protection. The Jews that moved to the castle seemed safe. However, outside of the castle walls, Jews still living in the city found themselves under attack as rioting, arson and the theft of Jewish property continued.

As the rioting continued, the Jews sheltering in the keep of the castle grew increasingly worried. They thought that the constable might let in the mob rioting outside. The constable left the castle and when he returned the Jews refused to let him in. The constable asked John Marshall, the Sheriff of Yorkshire, to help him. Marshall had a number of armed men with him and decided to remove the Jews from the castle by force. The sheriff's order to besiege the castle was a fatal decision. The rioting crowd took this as a sign that an attack on the Jews in the castle would have royal approval. They attacked the castle.

Remarkably the Jews were able to defend themselves for several days, helped by the strength of the castle's defences. On 16 March siege machines were moved into position. It now became obvious to the Jews that they could not hold out any longer. The Jews felt that they faced almost certain death. Many Jews committed suicide. Josce, the leader of the Jewish community, cut the throats of his wife, Anna, and his sons. It is thought that other Jewish fathers killed their wives and children, rather than face the rioters. At daybreak on the following morning those Jews that were still alive appealed for mercy. Their attackers said that they could leave the castle but that, in return for their safety, they must agree to be baptised as Christians. However, as they left the castle they were massacred. Their attackers had no intentions of keeping their promises.

Immediately after the massacre, many of the leaders of the riot made their way to York Minster where they seized Jewish documents relating to debts that were owed to Jewish moneylenders. These Jewish bonds were burned in the middle of the church.

When Richard heard news of the massacre he was angry and sent his chancellor, William de Longchamp, to England with orders to punish the rebels. William arrived in York on 3 May with a large number of troops. However, by the time he reached the city, many of the leaders of the massacre had fled. William dismissed the Sheriff of Yorkshire and the constable of York castle. He found it almost impossible to punish anyone else.

William imposed a series of heavy fines on the citizens of York. The amount that individuals had to pay was based on their wealth rather than their involvement in the riot. However, the general prejudice towards Jews made it difficult to bring anyone to trial. Some leaders of the massacre had their land confiscated. They had to pay the Crown a fine to get their land returned. Fines totalled £430.

2.7 Communicating your answer: Thinking about causation (part 1)

In your exam you will be asked to explain why events occurred. At the same time, we also want you to think about how to plan and write an effective answer to exam questions that focus on the key historical concept of **causation**.

Why did anti-Jewish pogroms occur in England in 1189–90?

The attack on Jews in York was not a one-off event. In 1189–90 anti-Jewish pogroms took place in towns and cities across England. You are now going to look at why these pogroms took place.

Look at the practice question below:

Explain why there were anti-Jewish pogroms in 1189–90. (12 marks)

There are two dangers with this type of question:

1 You only cover one cause of the event. The examiner will expect to see you cover a range of reasons.

2 You tell the story of *what* happened rather than explaining *why* the event happened.

Step 1: Using categories to help you think about causation

Careful planning is crucial for exam questions that ask you to explain why something happened. There are usually a range of reasons why events occur. One way to help you plan effectively is to sort the causes of an event into categories. Think about the history you have studied so far at school. What big factors are usually at work causing change?

We have provided four big factors below:

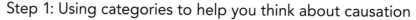

The attitudes and beliefs of people living at the time (in this case **religious** beliefs)	**Government** action (in this case the actions of the king and his royal government)	**Economic** causes	Short-term **triggers** (other events that happened in the lead up to event you are studying)

> Some of your exam questions (such as questions 5(b), 5(c) (i) and 5(c) (ii) in the exam paper) will suggest two topics you could use in your answer. You can see examples on page 112. We have not included topics in the practice questions in this book to give teachers the opportunity to change these from year to year.

Create a **Knowledge Organiser** by writing down each of these factors on a different sheet of paper. As you read through the information on page 27, record reasons why the anti-Jewish pogroms took place under the relevant heading. The great news is that you will be sorting the causes into categories as you go. You will use a range of Knowledge Organisers as you work through this book. They will help you focus on the key points and organise your notes.

Step 2: Deciding which causes are most important

When you finish you should find that you have identified three factors that played a major role in causing the anti-Jewish pogroms that took place. Each of these factors can form a paragraph in your answer. In your conclusion you need to decide which factor was the most important. Was it religious beliefs or are you going to argue that another factor was more important? It will help you if you discuss this with someone else – especially if they disagree with you and you have to debate what the main cause of the pogroms was.

Reasons for the pogroms

Growing anti-Semitism

Jews suffered from attacks and persecution in other European countries. They were often persecuted by Christians and blamed for the death of Jesus. This type of prejudice, hatred and discrimination against Jews, as a religious or racial group, is known as anti-Semitism. In England, anti-Semitism had been growing during the later years of Henry II's reign. As Jews became more involved in the economy, and some individual Jews grew rich, it provoked strong criticism, jealousy and anger.

Events at Richard I's coronation

Anti-Jewish feeling was increased by events at Richard I's coronation. On 3 September 1189, leading Jews joined Christians gathered at Westminster for the King's coronation. Several Jews tried to make their way into Westminster Palace during the coronation banquet as they had gifts for the King. This angered the crowd at the gate of the palace, and this anger turned into a full-scale anti-Jewish riot. Jewish homes were burned and it is estimated that at least 30 Jews lost their lives. Richard I was worried that anti-Jewish riots would spread from London to other cities. Richard regarded the Jews as an important source of royal revenue (see page 24). He sent messengers and letters throughout his kingdom ordering that they should be left in peace. Richard had some of the rioters arrested and three of them hanged.

The Crusades

Richard left England in December 1189, travelling to northern France where he stayed for six months. While he was on the Continent, knights and soldiers were coming together to prepare to set off on crusade. Propaganda encouraging Christians to join the crusade to recapture Jerusalem criticised Jews as well as Muslims. Saladin's conquest of Jerusalem shocked and angered Christians. Emotions were high and the Jews found themselves as scapegoats for attacks. There were outbreaks of violence in East Anglia during February 1190. Anti-Jewish riots took place in King's Lynn and Norwich. These spread to Stamford, Bury St Edmunds and Lincoln in March. The massacre of Jews in York (page 25) was therefore part of a pattern of vicious anti-Jewish riots that resulted in Jewish property being burned and Jewish people being murdered.

Other causes

The massacre of Jews in York seems to have had other causes as well. The rioters included a large number of men from the countryside as well as men from the city. Historians believe that many of the leaders of the riot were landlords who owed money to Jewish moneylenders. The Yorkshire knights who were involved in the attacks belonged to the middle rather than the higher levels of society. It seems as if some landlords were making a deliberate attempt to get rid of the evidence of their debts. During the pogrom they burned the books that kept records of debts owed to Jews. This prevented them being turned into debts for the Crown. The Yorkshire barons involved in the attack at York may therefore have had different motives to the labourers and young men who formed the mob.

Richard appears to have been angered by the massacre at York. He saw it as a challenge to his authority and he knew that this would lose money for the royal exchequer. The Jews of York were one of the richest Jewish communities in the country.

2.8 Visible learning: Review and revise

WHO REPRESENTED THE BIGGEST THREAT TO THE KING'S POSITION?

Having looked at English society in 1189, which group of people do you think represented the biggest threat to the king? Who did he really need to keep onside if he was going to govern the country effectively?

1 Form a hypothesis based on what you have found out in Chapters 1 and 2.

2 What words would you use to describe the threat posed by each of the groups listed in the cards below? Use the phrases and sentence starters from the word wall to help you form arguments and support them.

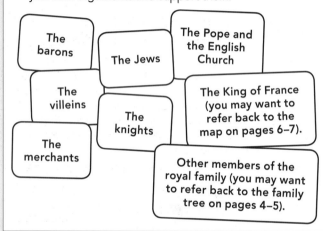

The barons

The Jews

The Pope and the English Church

The villeins

The knights

The King of France (you may want to refer back to the map on pages 6–7).

The merchants

Other members of the royal family (you may want to refer back to the family tree on pages 4–5).

Practice questions

Use the advice in the 'Writing better history' section of the book (see pages 112–122) to help you.

1 Describe two key features of knight service between 1189 and 1216.

2 Describe two key features of labour service between 1189 and 1216.

3 Describe two key features of agricultural life between 1189 and 1216.

4 Describe two key features of life in towns between 1189 and 1216.

5 Describe two key features of the role of a priest between 1189 and 1216.

6 Explain why religion was so important to people living between 1189 and 1216.

7 Explain why there were anti-Jewish pogroms in 1189–90.

8 'The Crusades were the main reason for the anti-Jewish pogroms in 1189–90.' How far do you agree? Explain your answer.

The word wall

In history it is important to vary your language to show how important you think a person, group, event (or a cause or consequence of an event) is. Use the word wall to help you find the right language to communicate your argument.

- The phrases in green help you to form a clear argument.
- Those in red help you support that argument.

Forming an argument:

… was the **most important/significant threat** to your position.

… was a **major/highly significant danger**.

… was an **important/considerable threat**.

… was of **some** threat to you.

… only posed a **limited/partial/slight** threat.

Supporting an argument

For example …

This can be seen when …

This is clearly shown by …

This is supported by …

This is proven by …

What can we learn from medieval monarchs before Richard and John?

People expected many things from their king and being a medieval monarch was not an easy job. This can be seen from the problems faced by Richard and John's predecessors. The kings who ruled England before Richard and John were all very different but they faced similar problems.

REVIEWING YOUR HYPOTHESIS

1 Use the information below to list the main problems that medieval monarchs faced between 1066 and 1189.

2 Review your hypothesis about who represented the biggest threat to Richard and John. Use the word wall on page 28 to help you find the right words and phrases to complete your argument.

1066 – WILLIAM I

William, Duke of Normandy faced a powerful rival for the throne. After the death of Edward the Confessor in 1066, Harold Godwinson, the most powerful man in England, claimed the throne. William invaded England and defeated Harold at the Battle of Hastings. He faced rebellions in different parts of the country but he gradually brought the whole country under his control. William's position as Duke of Normandy, as well as King of England, meant that England became closely connected with Europe. William fought against the King of France and also faced the threat of a Danish invasion. William died fighting in France.

1087 – WILLIAM II

The third son of William I was left the throne by his father and arrived in England before his brother could claim the throne. The barons rebelled during his reign. William II fought against Scotland and Wales, as well as France. He died after being shot by an arrow while out hunting. Some historians believe that this was no accident and that he may have been murdered by his younger brother, Henry, who was part of the hunting party and had a great deal to gain from his brother's death.

1100 – HENRY I

The youngest son of William I quickly claimed the throne after William II's death. Henry faced the threat of invasion from his elder brother, Robert, who also claimed the throne. Robert invaded in 1101, but Henry defeated him. Henry also fought against France. His only son, William, drowned in 1120 and Henry declared that his daughter, Matilda, should succeed him.

1135 – STEPHEN

The grandson of William I (the son of William's daughter). Stephen seized the throne when Henry I died in 1135. The throne had been promised to Matilda (Henry I's daughter). She was supported by some barons and invaded England. This caused a civil war that lasted for many years. Finally, it was agreed that Matilda's son (Henry) would become the next king when Stephen died.

1154 – HENRY II

Henry quarrelled with Thomas Becket, the Archbishop of Canterbury. Henry wanted to reduce the power of the Church courts but Becket opposed him. In 1170 Henry's anger spilled over and he shouted out 'Will no one rid me of this troublesome priest?' Four knights heard this. They burst into Canterbury Cathedral and murdered Becket. Henry was blamed for Becket's death and it damaged his reputation.

Some leading barons joined with the King of Scotland and rebelled against Henry in 1173. Henry kept strong control over the barons. He destroyed many of their castles and built royal castles in places where they were a major threat. However, Henry's main problem was the difficulty he faced in keeping control of his own family. His sons rebelled against him in 1173, 1183 and 1189.

3 Kingship, succession and royal government

By now you should have built up a clear picture of English society and the main threats to medieval monarchs. This chapter focuses on the main duties and challenges facing Richard and John as medieval monarchs. You will compare how Richard and John secured the throne, governed England and raised money.

3.1 What was the nature of medieval kingship?

Rights, rituals and display

The coronation ceremony

This ceremony was a very important ritual. Kings were crowned at Westminster Abbey. On coronation day the king was led by a procession of clergy to the high altar. At the heart of the ceremony was the deeply religious act of anointing the king with sanctified 'holy oil'. This symbolised the part which God and his Church played in king-making in medieval England. The king was not fully or lawfully king until he was crowned. It was only with the crowning that God's approval was unmistakeable and royal acts were given authority.

The king had to take a triple oath which expressed the duties of kingship: to protect the Church, to offer justice to all and to act with mercy.

The act of homage

Following the blessing of the day's events and the crowned king, those present swore homage to the king (see page 15). The swearing of homage by his tenants-in-chief acknowledged the rights possessed by an English king – ultimately, that the king owned all the land in the kingdom.

Display

Important objects symbolised some of the key features of medieval kingship:

- The orb – a symbol of the king's rights and responsibilities as a ruler.
- The sceptre – symbolising the king's role as a judge.
- The ring – 'the seal of holy faith'.
- The sword – implying protection of his kingdom and people.
- The crown representing the glory of kingship. At his coronation, Richard I took the heavy gold crown himself from the high altar and handed it to the Archbishop of Canterbury for the actual crowning. The King often wore a crown at religious festivals. This reminded the king's people that he was their duly crowned and anointed king and re-emphasised the importance of the coronation.

◀ This picture shows the coronation of a medieval English king, believed to be Edward III. He is seated on a coronation chair and is surrounded by members of the royal court, the Archbishop of Canterbury, priests and lawyers.

What were the main duties and responsibilities of a king?

It was believed that kings were chosen by God to protect and govern their people. The king was God's chosen representative on Earth. He had a role as a judge, priest and knight. He also had to manage the barons effectively and this meant providing strong but fair government. These five roles are shown in the cartoon below.

THE NATURE OF MEDIEVAL KINGSHIP

1 Describe the main features of the coronation ceremony for a medieval monarch.

2 Explain the main duties of a medieval monarch.

Knight: The king was in charge of the royal army. He led it into battle. He had to be a brave and successful soldier to win respect, land and to defend the country from the threat of invasion.

Governor: People believed that kings had a duty to govern well. The king made most of the key decisions, but he needed to appoint skilled people to help him run the country. The king also needed to raise a lot of money because he was expected to look the part and impress people by displaying wealth and power through his royal court. He also often faced threats from other monarchs, and it was important to be able to raise a large army when needed. Raising and equipping an army were very expensive.

Judge: The king had to settle disputes and punish people who broke the law. He put people on trial in his own court, or sent his judges around the country to settle cases for him. People expected the courts and the king to be fair.

Priest: Religion was an important part of everyone's life. People believed that the king had been chosen by God to rule over them. They expected the king to protect, support and respect the Church.

Manager: The king made the key decisions but he was expected to consult with his leading barons. A successful monarch needed to win the support of the barons by establishing law and order, communicating with them clearly, and making them feel safe and secure.

What qualities did a medieval monarch need to be successful?

As you can see, people in the Middle Ages expected a great deal of their king. A successful king needed certain qualities to succeed. What do you think they were? Remember not to be anachronistic by thinking of qualities a successful leader would need today. Look at this through the eyes of a medieval baron!

A GOOD KING WAS …

1 Look at the list on the right. What qualities do you think were the most important? Choose three qualities from the list and explain how they would help a king be successful.

2 Extra Challenge – play the A–Z game. Aim to think of as many qualities as possible that start with a different letter of the alphabet.

lazy	honest
funny	greedy
good looking	healthy
educated	fair
musical	hardworking
brave	charismatic
cruel	popular
religious	respectful
ruthless	thoughtful
cunning	tactical

3.2 Was Richard better prepared than John to rule the Angevin Empire?

In Chapter 1 we looked at some of the historical interpretations that have been constructed about Richard and John. One interpretation is that Richard's character, skills and experiences meant that he was far more likely to be successful than John. You need to test this interpretation and reach your own judgement.

This is an artist's impression of what Richard looked like.

RICHARD I

PERSONAL DETAILS
- Born on 8 September 1157 in Oxford, England.
- Oldest surviving son of Henry II.
- Brought up by his mother (Eleanor of Aquitaine) and his nurse (Hodierna).
- Spent much of his early life in the Duchy of Aquitaine.
- Educated in Latin and trained in the art of war.
- Interested in words and music – a songwriter and poet.
- Interested in other cultures.

CHARACTER AND PERSONALITY
- Intelligent with a good sense of humour.
- Charismatic – other men seemed willing to follow him.
- Stubborn – for example, in 1174, having rebelled against his father, Richard fought on despite the loss of 60 knights and 400 archers.
- Arrogant and over-confident – he seemed to think that there was no problem he could not solve. His arrogance meant that he made some enemies without realising it.
- Ruthless and at times cruel – according to Gervase of Canterbury, 'the great nobles of Aquitaine hated him because of his great cruelty'.
- Very brave – willing to put his own life at risk in battle. This could also be seen as recklessness.
- Cunning – could take enemies by surprise by launching unexpected attacks.
- A supremely effective soldier – impressed his own men and enemy troops.

EXPERIENCES
- 1172 – At the age of just 14, Richard was formally installed as Duke of Aquitaine.
- 1173 – Joined his mother and brothers (Henry and Geoffrey) in rebellion against their father; defeated by Henry II.
- 1175 – A rebellion broke out in Aquitaine. Richard was given full control of the Duchy of Aquitaine's armed forces and given orders to punish rebels and bring Aquitaine under control.
- 1176–77 – Richard quickly defeated the rebels in Aquitaine.
- 1179 – Some barons in Aquitaine rebelled. Richard showed himself to be an expert in the art of siege warfare when he captured Taillebourg from Geoffrey de Rancon. This impressed people at the time because very few people believed that Taillebourg could be taken as it was so well protected.
- 1181–88 – Further rebellions broke out in Aquitaine in 1181 and 1188 but Richard was able to keep control and defeat the rebels.
- 1183 – Fought alongside his father when the young Henry and Geoffrey rebelled once again against their father.
- 1183–84 – By the end of 1183, the young Henry had died and Richard was in a new position as Henry's chief heir. During the winter of 1183, Henry II tried to persuade Richard to give Aquitaine to John. When Richard refused, John joined forces with Geoffrey and tried to invade Aquitaine. Richard was able to defend his lands.
- 1189 – Went to war against Henry II who seemed to be favouring John as his heir. Many barons supported Richard, who joined forces with Philip II, the King of France.
- 1189 – Richard becomes king.

WHO WAS BETTER PREPARED TO BE KING?

1 Use the information outlining Richard and John's experiences before they became king on pages 32–33 to fill in the Knowledge Organiser below.

2 Use your completed table to reach a judgement. Was Richard more likely to succeed as ruler of the Angevin Empire? Compare their characters, skills and experiences to decide.

Criteria	Richard	John
Personality and character What qualities do they have that are useful? Are there any personal traits that could cause a problem?		
Military experience Will they be able to defeat rivals for the throne or threats from other kings?		
Experience of government Have they got a good track record of governing effectively?		

KING JOHN

PERSONAL DETAILS

- Born in Oxford in 1167.
- Fourth son of Henry II and Eleanor of Aquitaine – his father's favourite son.
- As he was Henry's fourth eldest son, it was not expected that he would become king. John's three elder brothers would have learned the skills of a knight. John had far less military training and was probably being prepared for a career in the Church.
- Interested in the law and books (had a large library of French and Latin books).

This is an artist's impression of what John looked like

CHARACTER AND PERSONALITY

- Intelligent and hard working.
- Bad tempered and cruel.
- Insecure and suspicious of others – found it difficult to trust people ... and people found it difficult to trust him.
- Devious and disloyal.

EXPERIENCES

- 1177 – Henry II apponted him King of Ireland (John did not visit until 1185).
- 1183 – John went to war against Richard (who had refused Henry II's request for him to hand over Aquitaine to John).
- 1185 – John travelled to Ireland. It was rumoured that men in John's party showed little respect to the Irish lords and even pulled them by their beards! John tended to listen to the younger men who travelled with him rather than the more experienced men who had worked for Henry II. John rewarded his own followers and friends. The local Irish lords rebelled against him. John suffered several defeats and was forced to return home.
- 1189 – John joined Richard's side in a war against his father. When Richard became king, John was made the custodian of Cornwall, Dorset, Somerset, Nottingham, Derby and Lancaster.
- 1190 – When Richard left for the crusade, William de Longchamp was placed in charge of England. John was made to swear an oath not to enter England without first seeking Richard's permission.
- 1192 – Richard was captured and imprisoned on his journey home from the crusade. John formed an alliance with Philip II of France and plotted against his brother. He spread rumours that Richard was dead and moved to seize Richard's lands in England. Richard's supporters remained loyal and laid siege to John's castles. When Richard returned, John threw himself at Richard's feet for mercy.
- 1195 – Richard eventually forgave John and allowed him to take control of his former properties.
- 1196 – John joined Richard's army in France, fighting against Philip II.
- 1199 – John becomes king.

3.3 Securing the throne

Medieval monarchs often had to fight to secure the throne. When a king died the succession was often disputed (look back at page 29 and remind yourself of all the conflicts caused by competing claims for the throne). It was not until later in the Middle Ages that the idea that the eldest son should inherit the throne became more accepted and the dying wishes of the old king were not always followed. Edward Confessor named Harold as his heir, Henry I wanted Matilda to take power – on both occasions rivals seized the throne.

Some historians have argued that John was unlucky as he faced greater problems than Richard. One of the ways they support this interpretation is by arguing that

John had to fight harder than Richard to secure the throne.

DID JOHN HAVE TO FIGHT HARDER THAN RICHARD TO SECURE THE THRONE?

1 As you read pages 34–35, use the Knowledge Organiser below to collect evidence that supports or counters (goes against) this interpretation.

2 Reach a judgement – how far do you agree that 'John had to fight harder to secure the throne'?

Evidence to support the statement 'John had to fight harder than Richard to secure the throne'	Evidence that counters the statement 'John had to fight harder than Richard to secure the throne'

Richard's claim to the throne

- Richard was the oldest surviving son of Henry II.
- Only one other son (John) was still alive.

How did Richard secure power?

Richard was very worried that his father would name John as his heir. John was Henry II's favourite son, while Richard had rebelled against his father in the past. Philip II, the King of France, saw an opportunity to cause problems for Henry II. He was able to play upon Richard's fears. Philip encouraged Richard to push his claim to the throne. In 1189 they made a series of demands to Henry:

- Richard should be allowed to marry Philip's sister (Alice).
- Henry should acknowledge Richard as the heir to the Angevin Empire.
- John should join the crusade to the Holy Land.

When Henry rejected these terms, Philip and Richard launched a surprise attack on Henry's lands on the Continent, successfully capturing Maine and Touraine. On 4 July, Henry met Philip and Richard and agreed to peace terms. Henry agreed that his subjects both in England and in France were to swear allegiance to Richard. He also promised to pay Philip 20,000 marks. Henry died two days later and Richard became king. Henry's last hours were made even worse by the news that during Richard and Philip's attacks on his lands, John had deserted his father and joined his brother's side.

John's claim to the throne

- John's older brother, Richard, died without any children.
- John was the only surviving son of Henry II.
- John's nephew, Arthur (the son of John's older brother Geoffrey), also claimed the throne. Arthur was the young Duke of Brittany and had the support of the barons of Anjou, Maine, and Touraine (see map below).

How did John secure power?

In 1197 Richard confirmed that John was his preferred successor. When Richard died, the key men in Normandy and England quickly showed their support for John. In Aquitaine, Eleanor guaranteed that the duchy would go to John. However, the leading men in Brittany chose Arthur as their new ruler, as did most of the key men in Anjou, Maine and Touraine.

To make matters worse for John, soon after Richard's death, Philip II invaded Normandy. John acted with impressive speed and was quick to get his authority recognised in Normandy and England. On 27 May he was crowned king at Westminster, and by the end of June he was back in Rouen with a large army.

Arthur posed a significant threat to John. In the minds of some people, he had a better claim than John to be Richard's successor. Arthur had paid homage to Philip and had the resources of the French monarch on his side.

Between 1199 and 1202 John spent much of his time on the Continent securing control of his lands and combating the threat posed by Arthur. John was able to force Philip to retreat and benefited when Arthur's key supporter in Anjou, William des Roches, decided to change sides. John also gained the valuable support of the Count of Angouleme when he ended his marriage to Isabella of Gloucester and married the Count's daughter (also called Isabella). The city of Angouleme was crucial for John's control of Poitou. Bringing the Count of Angouleme on his side by marrying his daughter made good sense.

In May 1200 John made peace with Philip through the Treaty of Le Goulet (see box). The settlement with Philip brought two years of peace and meant that John's position as ruler of the Angevin Empire had been secured.

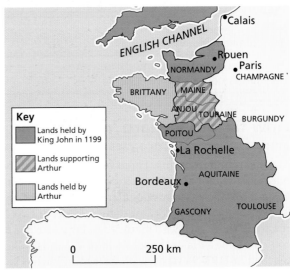

▲ This map shows the lands held by John when he became King in 1199 and the lands that supported Arthur.

THE TERMS OF THE TREATY OF LE GOULET

- Philip recognised John as Richard's heir and John's right to all his Continental possessions.
- It was agreed Arthur could hold the Duchy of Brittany but John would be his overlord. The following day John received Arthur's homage for Brittany.
- The treaty laid down a clear boundary between Normandy and France. Philip gained some land on the border between Normandy and France but John remained in control of the key areas.
- John agreed to pay Philip the massive sum of 20,000 marks for his Continental territories. This was in recognition of his feudal relationship (payment of relief) with Philip as his overlord.

3.4 Who governed more effectively – Richard or John?

Having secured power, Richard and John faced the challenge of governing the Angevin Empire. We look at how they ruled over their lands in Normandy in Chapter 5, but here we focus on how they governed England. This is an area of considerable debate between historians.

- Richard has been criticised for neglecting the government of England. However, some historians have argued that this is an unfair claim and that he made good decisions and played as active a role as was possible in royal government.
- John has been praised for being 'an energetic and skilled administrator'. However, some historians have criticised John's key decisions, such as his choice of advisers.

WHO GOVERNED MORE EFFECTIVELY?

?

It is time for you to join the debate. Use the information on pages 36–37 to test the two interpretations in the Knowledge Organiser below. After you have filled in the table, write a short paragraph explaining who you think governed England more effectively.

Interpretation	Evidence to support	Evidence to counter
Richard neglected the government of England.		
John was an energetic and skilled administrator.		

How far did Richard 'neglect' the government of England?

At the start of his reign Richard had Henry II's most unpopular **ministers** arrested and dragged round in chains. Those who Henry had imprisoned without a proper trial were released. Richard also restored the land of all those that his father had disinherited. His policies increased his popularity. Gervase of Canterbury commented that Richard 'spoke kindly to all that came to him. Hence at first he was much loved'. Richard skilfully rewarded those men who mattered, taking care not to offend or disappoint barons who could become a major threat. Richard's success is shown by the fact that when John rebelled in 1193–94 very few of the leading barons supported him.

Use of patronage

Kings at the time could give gifts of land and important **offices** to their followers on a large scale. This gave kings a great deal of power. The careful management of this vast system of **patronage** was an essential part of being an effective king. Richard used these powers very cleverly. On becoming king, Richard pardoned Henry's most loyal followers. Instead of punishing powerful men like William Marshal he worked hard to get them onside. William had once come close to killing Richard in battle but Richard forgave him and gave him lands in Wales and Ireland.

Richard was able to draw the great knights of the time to his side and use them to his advantage. For example, Richard gave William (a highly skilled military commander) land in Wales because he was worried about the threat posed there by Lord Rhys, the powerful Welsh prince. Richard also returned land to Robert, Earl of Leicester, that Henry II had taken away. Robert was an excellent soldier and he became a key figure in the defence of Richard's lands in Normandy.

Securing England's borders

One of Richard's main aims early in his reign was to make sure that England's borders were safe. Richard met the leading Welsh kings, who promised not to attack England while he was on crusade. The Welsh kings kept their promises. None of them interfered in English politics when John led a rebellion against Richard in 1193–94. Richard also made a lasting peace agreement with William 'The Lion', King of Scotland. He formally acknowledged Scotland's independence from England. In return William paid 10,000 marks and remained loyal to Richard. The money helped to pay for Richard's crusade.

How was England governed when Richard was absent?

Richard has been criticised for being obsessed with war and having little interest in the government of England. It is true that Richard spent little time in the country. He left England in 1190, first heading to Normandy and then joining the crusade to the Holy Land in the Middle East. Richard did not return to England until 1194, by which time John had rebelled and Philip had attacked his lands on the Continent. In May 1194, Richard left England again – this time to fight Philip II and attempt to regain his lands in France. Richard never returned to England.

While Richard was in France he left England in the hands of Hubert Walter, who had served with Richard on the crusade. Walter was a very capable administrator and had gained a great deal of experience under Henry II. He was also well respected and had been elected Archbishop of Canterbury in 1193.

Richard and Walter were able to put in place a strong system of government that did not need to be constantly supervised by the king in person. Letters and documents from his reign show that Richard kept up to date with what was going on in England. He kept strong control over the English Church, making sure that his own men became bishops. Key laws still required the King's authorisation. Although Richard spent the last five years of his reign on the Continent, for most of that time he was based in Normandy and from here it was easy to continue to control business in England.

▲ Statue of Hubert Walter from the exterior of Canterbury Cathedral.

How was England governed under John?

John inherited from Richard a detailed and effective administrative system – capable of functioning in his absence and raising large sums in revenue. Its effectiveness can be seen from the large sums of money it was able to raise, firstly to pay for Richard's crusade, then his ransom and finally his war against Philip II.

At first John kept most of Richard's key advisers in place. However, over time he replaced them with his own followers and friends. John's followers, many of them from France, were placed in important positions at the expense of leading English barons. This caused anger, jealousy and resentment. It also meant that John's system of government had a very narrow support base. John does not seem to have trusted his English barons, nor did he work as hard as Richard to win their support and loyalty. John failed to use his powers of patronage effectively. It was not long before John's enemies among the barons far outnumbered his friends.

In contrast to Richard, John spent most of his time in England. This was because by 1204 John had lost his lands in Normandy to Philip II. John spent most of his time on the move around the country. He personally attended many important court cases and regularly met and consulted his sheriffs. John was energetic and hardworking, a master of detail and personally oversaw the day-to-day running of the country. Historians have praised him for the way he reformed royal government and improved administration.

However, it should be remembered that John's improvements in government were driven by the need for money. The more efficient he made the system of royal government the more money he could raise to fund his plans to regain the land he had lost in France.

3.5 Finance: Did Richard and John make unreasonable financial demands?

A common criticism of both Richard and John is that they taxed England too heavily and made unreasonable financial demands. The word 'unreasonable' is important. People expected to contribute to royal revenues and pay taxes. However, leading barons would quickly become angry if they thought these taxes were too high or were not being introduced for a good reason.

RAISING TAXES – PART 1: 1189–1206 **?**

Read pages 38–39.

1 List the reasons why Richard and John needed to raise taxes.

2 Put yourself in the position of a leading baron.
   a) Do you think that Richard and John had good reasons for raising taxes?
   b) Look at the pie chart. Which ways of raising royal revenues would you dislike the most? Choose three methods and explain why leading barons would not like extra money to be raised in this way.
   c) Look at how Richard raised extra revenue when he really needed to. Do you think that the barons would have found these extra financial demands unreasonable? Explain your answer.

1189–1206: Why did Richard and John need to raise taxes?

The main reason that both Richard and John had to increase taxes was to pay for military expeditions overseas.

■ Richard – to pay for his crusade and then to win back his land in France (taken by Philip II while Richard was captured returning from crusade).

■ John – to defend his lands in France – which were being attacked by Philip II.

Kings had a small permanent army which was made up of around a hundred household knights. These highly skilled, professional soldiers formed the core of royal armies. Kings could also call on their soldiers based in the royal castles. When forming an army, the king also summoned his tenants-in-chief to provide him with knights. However, to fight overseas, kings needed to raise a large army and they often recruited professional soldiers from abroad (known as mercenary soldiers). An army also had to be equipped and supplied. All of this was very expensive.

How did Richard and John raise royal revenues?

At the start of his reign John's financial demands were similar to those made by Richard in the final years of his reign. The pie chart gives you an idea of how Richard and John raised royal revenues.

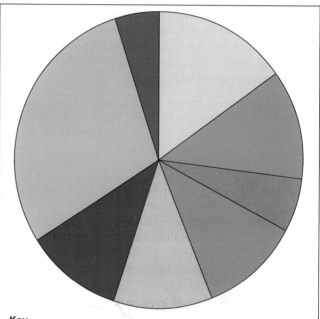

Key

☐ The county farm (15%) – revenues (collected by sheriffs) from the king's own land in the county. A fixed sum was expected.

☐ Taxes paid by the cities and boroughs (12%).

☐ The royal forest (6%) – large areas of the country were part of the royal forest and therefore under forest laws. Fines could be imposed for poaching or hunting deer and boar. People could also be fined for putting up buildings, cutting down trees and using the land to grow crops. These restrictions affected rich and poor.

☐ Tallages (11%) – these were general taxes, usually payable by everyone. Sometimes just the Jews were made to pay a tallage – the king could tax them as he wished.

☐ Feudal incidents (11%) – came from the relationship between the king and his tenants-in-chief. These revenues included money made from aids, reliefs and wardships.

☐ Scutage (11%) – paid by the tenants-in-chief in place of providing the king with military service. The amount a baron paid depended on how many knights he owed. In 1210 the amount rose to 10 marks per knight.

☐ Profits from justice (29%) – criminal justice brought a great deal of profit to the Crown. The property of criminals could be sold and the Crown had the right to hold their land and profit from it for one year. Numerous fines were imposed as punishments. Fines for committing an offence were known as amercements.

☐ Favours (5%) – offers of money accepted by the king for concessions or favours (for example, permission to start a legal action).

How did Richard raise extra revenue when he really needed to?

Richard's crusade put a lot of pressure on government finances. The records show the massive scale of Richard's preparations. His officials went from port to port, buying the biggest and best ships. Richard also had to pay the wages of the crews and the ships had to be fully supplied. How did Richard raise the vast sums of money he needed?

Selling offices and privileges

The king could choose who he wanted to help him run the country. Ambitious men were willing to offer large sums for privileges and offices from which they could profit. After he became king, Richard put almost everything he could offer up for sale. It was perfectly usual for offices (such as the position of sheriff), charters and privileges to be bought and sold, but this was normally spread over a number of years. In order to meet the financial demands of the crusade, Richard concentrated this into just one year.

Raising taxes

For his crusade, for his ransom, and then for his war against Philip, Richard made heavy financial demands on his subjects by requiring everyone in the kingdom to pay an aid (see box). After his release from captivity, Richard used more traditional methods to raise money such as scutages and reliefs. In 1194, in order to help pay for his expedition to Normandy, Richard introduced a scutage that raised just over £2,000. In addition, men who had bought offices in 1189 were informed that they had only gained them for a fixed period and they now had to pay again.

By the end of 1198 there was some discontent in England at the weight of Richard's financial demands. Richard had taxed more heavily than his father. However, much as people in England disliked the level of Richard's demands, there seems to have been an acceptance of the need to raise large sums of money. The crusade was seen as a religious duty while in 1194 people could see that it was necessary and only right that Richard should put all of his efforts into recovering the lands that Philip had taken. The fact that Richard was successful in his war against Philip also helped to ensure that there were no major protests about Richard's taxes.

SPECIAL CIRCUMSTANCES

In special circumstances a king could levy an aid. This was a general tax paid by everyone in the kingdom. People had to pay 25 per cent of the value of all their rents and moveables (this referred to peoples' movable property – mainly corn and farm animals). An aid was essentially a tax on property and the feudal custom allowed a lord to take an aid in three cases: the knighting of his first born son; the marriage of his first born daughter; to pay for his ransom if captured by enemies.

? Explain why sheriffs played an important role in helping Richard and John govern the country and collecting revenues.

THE ROLE OF SHERIFFS

England was divided into counties. Nearly all of the counties were under the control of sheriffs who were appointed and dismissed by the king. Sheriffs played an important role in local government and in collecting royal revenues.

- The king did not pass all his land on to tenants. The crown had many manors in every county. This land was known as the royal demesne (see page 14). It let this land out to sheriffs who managed the land for a lump sum – taking whatever money was made above that as a profit.
- Sheriffs had to collect revenues from manors in the county that formed part of the royal demesne. If a debtor did not pay, the sheriff could force the payment by seizing and selling the debtor's possessions.
- Sheriffs also helped to keep law and order. They presided over the county courts, arrested and hanged criminals, organised juries and enforced judgements.

How did John raise extra money in 1207–14?

By 1204 John had lost Normandy to Philip II. John was determined to win it back and from 1207 he started to increase the amount of money he demanded from his subjects, in order to build up a large army that could defeat Philip. From 1207 we see a real change in John's financial policies. Between 1199 and 1202 English revenues averaged £24,000 a year. Between 1207 and 1214 an average of £49,000 was raised each year.

By 1214 John had saved up £130,000. John's financial policies hit his barons hardest of all. Under Richard, there was a real sense that payments towards the ransom and crusade, though burdensome, were made in a good cause. Under John it was different and there was much resentment at John's financial policies as more and more barons fell into debt.

RAISING TAXES – PART 2: 1207–14 ?

1 Put yourself in the position of a leading baron again.
   a) Why might you be less willing to accept John increasing taxes than Richard?
   b) Look at how John raised the extra funds below. Which methods would annoy you the most? Choose three methods and explain why they would make the barons feel that John was making unreasonable demands.

2 Return to the main question and make a judgement – Did *both* Richard and John make unreasonable financial demands? Explain your main reasons for reaching this judgement.

How did John raise extra funds?

1 Sheriffs were expected to collect more revenue from the counties. This put extra pressure on the sheriffs who in turn placed extra financial pressure on people in the counties. Many sheriffs became unpopular because they exploited people in the area they controlled, seizing wood, property and even threatening people with trial unless they paid a bribe to be let off.

2 John levied aids which were paid by everyone who had anything worth taxing. These were only usually levied in special circumstances (for example, aids had been raised to pay Richard's ransom). In 1207, John asked that an aid might now be paid to defend the kingdom against the threat from Philip II and to recover his lands in France. The tax of 1207 produced an income of £57,000. The rate was to be paid at a thirteenth of the value of both rents and movables. Known as the Thirteenth, it was met with a lot of opposition and resistance. People tried to hide their possessions in monasteries and royal officers carried out raids to try and find them. It was assessed by a group of judges who were sent round the country. Anyone found guilty of concealment or false valuation lost all their moveables and was thrown in prison. This tax hit all sections of society.

3 John introduced more scutages than had been paid under his father and brother. Henry had levied 8 in 34 years and Richard 3 in 10 years. John levied 11 in 16 years.

4 In 1210 John introduced a large tax on the Jews. They were forced to pay £44,000.

5 The King increased the taxes paid by towns and cities. The tallage levied on towns and cities in 1210 raised over £10,000.

6 John introduced new policies to increase revenue from the royal forest. Large amounts of money (an estimated £9,000) were raised from heavy fines after 1207.

7 The King's judges also raised money when they visited the counties – seizing the chattels of convicted criminals and outlaws. Revenues from punishments more than trebled between 1209 and 1212.

8 John made sure that the Exchequer worked hard to calculate exactly what individual barons owed. Their debts were added together in one lump sum and they came under pressure to pay back their debts in a specific time period. John seized barons' lands as punishment if they failed to pay their debt on time.

9 John also demanded money from the widows of his tenants-in-chief. For example, in 1208, John stated that if Avelina, widow of Osbert de Longchamp, did not wish to marry Walter of Tew (one of John's household knights), Walter was to have her inheritance anyway. Avelina had to offer 500 marks to escape the marriage.

3.6 Visible learning: revise and remember

Successful students regularly review what they have been learning and plan their revision while they are studying. They do not leave revision until close to the exam. This page starts that revision process.

Review Key topic 1: Life and government in England, 1189–1216

It is important to regularly return to the big question we asked in Chapter 1:

What reputation does each king deserve?

By now you should have a good understanding of English society and what people at the time expected from their king. Use this knowledge and what you have learned so far to reflect on the different interpretations of Richard and John. How much evidence do you have already to support or counter the following statements made by supporters and critics of Richard and John?

Richard's reputation

Critics claim that he ...	Supporters claim that he ...
neglected the kingdom and raised unnecessarily high taxes.	set up a strong system of government and followed an appropriate financial policy.
lacked political wisdom, angered the barons and made rushed decisions.	was a clever politician who managed the Church and the barons effectively.
was obsessed with war and wasted England's resources fighting pointless wars overseas.	was a military genius who fought wars that were seen as his duty or were fought to protect his Empire.

John's reputation

Critics claim that he ...	Supporters claim that he ...
made mistakes in government and raised unnecessarily high taxes.	was an intelligent and hardworking king who improved royal government and finances.
was an arrogant, cruel and aggressive ruler who failed to manage his barons effectively.	was unlucky and faced major problems.
was a military failure who lacked boldness and made mistakes when leading his army.	managed to secure the throne and had some military successes.

Revise and remember

You need to work at making your knowledge stick in your brain. The more you recap what you have learned and identify what you're not sure about, the more chance you have of success.

Challenge

Do you know what these key words or phrases mean?

tenant-in-chief	merchant
free tenant	purgatory
villein	anti-Semitism
a relief	an aid
rights of wardship	an amercement
a manor	scutage

Practice questions

Use the advice in the 'Writing better history' section of the book (see pages 112–122) to help you.

1 Describe two key features of the coronation ceremony for a medieval monarch.
2 Describe two key features of the role of a sheriff between 1189 and 1216.
3 Explain the main duties of a medieval monarch.
4 Explain why Richard and John had to raise taxes.
5 'Richard neglected the government of England'. How far do you agree? Explain your answer.
6 'John had to fight harder than Richard to secure the throne.' How far do you agree? Explain your answer.

The actions overseas of Richard and John went a long way to define their reputations among their contemporaries. Medieval chroniclers praised Richard's bravery and military successes on crusade, while John's failure to defend Normandy led to him being given the nickname 'soft-sword'. In this key topic you will explore the key events that Richard and John became involved in overseas between 1189 and 1204.

In Chapter 4 you will look at:

- the reasons why Richard joined the Third Crusade
- the nature of the crusading army
- the main battles that Richard fought and the important decisions he had to take
- the impact of Richard's crusade and how it affected England.

In Chapter 5 you will focus on Normandy and look at:

- the competing aims of Philip II (the King of France), Richard and John
- Richard's successful defence of Normandy
- the reasons why John had lost Normandy by 1204.

4.1 Warfare overseas

Warfare was a major part of life in the Middle Ages. As you have seen in Chapter 2, a king who failed as a military leader could quickly lose the respect and support of his people. In Chapter 3 you explored royal finances – fighting wars was very expensive and brought enormous financial pressure. The loss of land to another country meant a loss of resources and further financial problems. All of this meant that a king who failed in battle was likely to fail as king.

Recently, some historians have challenged the interpretations of Richard and John's record overseas. They have argued that John's failures have been over-exaggerated – that he was unlucky and deserves 'some sympathy' for the loss of Normandy. Others have queried whether Richard's crusade was a success, criticising him for his failure to recapture Jerusalem and his brutal treatment of prisoners.

THE BIG QUESTIONS

In Chapters 4 and 5 you will form your own opinions of Richard and John as military leaders. Try and keep these key questions in mind:

- Was Richard a 'military genius' or have his achievements overseas been over-exaggerated?
- Was John a poor soldier or did he face 'impossible difficulties' in defending the Angevin Empire overseas?

Representations of Richard ▶
and John in books often reflect
the views expressed in the
medieval chronicles.

4.2 Why did so many people join the Third Crusade?

Richard I was not the first Christian king to join a crusade. In this enquiry you will briefly explore previous crusades, the nature of crusading and the immediate causes and events leading up to the Third Crusade. You will analyse Richard's aims and motives for joining the Crusade, as well as those of the thousands of people who joined him from England and western Europe.

BACKGROUND TO THE THIRD CRUSADE

As you read pages 43–45 make brief notes on:

- how the concept of crusading began
- the nature of crusading – who joined the crusades? Where did they fight?
- reasons why people joined the First and Second Crusades
- reasons why Saladin was able to take control of Jerusalem.

How did the concept of crusade begin?

The crusades were wars between Christians and non-Christians. The most famous crusades were fought against Muslim armies in the area around Jerusalem. Our study starts at the end of the eleventh century with the beginning of the concept of a crusade.

Stage 1: The First Crusade

In 1095 Pope Urban II called on Christians in western Europe to travel East and fight against a group of Muslims called the Seljuk Turks. He claimed that they were persecuting Christians and stopping them from visiting the holy city of Jerusalem where Christ had been crucified.

The Pope promised that anyone who fought to free Jerusalem from Muslim control would be rewarded with a place in Heaven. His message was very powerful, and somewhere between 50,000 and 100,000 Christians set off to the Holy Land. This was probably the largest army Europe had seen since the days of the Roman Empire. Jerusalem was taken in 1099. Many of the inhabitants of the city were massacred as the victorious Christians rampaged through the city taking gold, silver, horses and other possessions. Jews were burned in their synagogue, while many Muslims were tortured. It is hard to be sure how many Muslims were killed. Some historians argue around 3,000, while others think that as many as 10,000 may have been killed.

Although there was rivalry and disagreements between the different European princes who led the crusade, the army was well motivated. Even the poorest of the crusaders earned a large sum of money for their part in the attack on Jerusalem. However, what seems to have driven most crusaders on was the hope of an easier passage to Heaven. Pope Urban II promised, as God's representative on Earth, that going on crusade and fighting in a war against enemies of the Church would bring a full indulgence. This was what every Christian, rich or poor, wanted – a promise of complete forgiveness so that your soul could pass straight to Heaven without having to go through Purgatory.

▲ The capture of Jerusalem in 1099, from a fourteenth-century French biography of Godfrey of Bouillon.

THINK BACK AND CONNECT

Look back at pages 22–23. Why was a full indulgence so important to people in the Middle Ages?

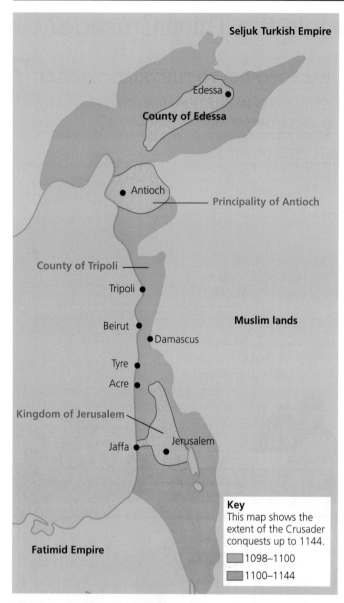

▲ This map shows the extent of the crusader conquests up to 1144.

Key
This map shows the extent of the Crusader conquests up to 1144.
☐ 1098–1100
☐ 1100–1144

▲ A late medieval picture of Saladin.

Stage 2: Christian control of the Holy Land grows

For the first half of the twelfth century, the crusaders controlled Jerusalem and a thin strip of land along the coast. This made them vulnerable to attack, therefore the crusaders fought to win more lands until they were all part of one connected kingdom. The Muslims were unable to stop them because they were not united. They were more interested in fighting each other. There were also religious divisions between Sunni Muslims (like the Abbasids and the Seljuk Turks) and Shi'ite Muslims (like the Fatimid ruling family in Egypt).

The Fatimids were keen to gain greater control over the lands held by the Seljuk Turks, even if it meant fighting fellow Muslims. Many crusaders stayed and settled in the Kingdom of Jerusalem, changing the way they lived to fit in with the climate. They also picked up new ideas about house building and medicine from their Muslim neighbours.

Stage 3: The Muslims fight back

In 1144 Muslims, led by Imad ad-Din Zengi, recaptured the crusader lands around Edessa, massacring Christians who lived there. Zengi had a reputation as a fearsome and ruthless warrior. Generals who angered him were exiled and their sons castrated. Soldiers who marched out of line were crucified.

Zengi's capture of Edessa led the Christians living in the crusader states to ask for help from the West. In 1147, a second crusade set off east, comprising two armies led by two of the most powerful Kings of Europe: Conrad III of Germany and Louis VII of France. The King of France was accompanied by his wife at the time – Eleanor of Aquitaine – who was mother to Richard and John (see page 5).

The Second Crusade ended in failure. The crusaders were regularly attacked as they crossed Anatolia by Seljuk Turk forces. Both armies suffered terrible losses, and by the time they arrived in the Holy Land, Edessa had been destroyed. The crusaders launched an attack on Damascus but the siege was unsuccessful. They had failed to defeat the Muslim forces and returned to Europe humiliated.

During the second half of the twelfth century, Nur ad-Din (Zengi's son) gained control of Syria, uniting the Muslims living there. Between 1163 and 1174 he and his generals took control of Egypt. The crusader states were now surrounded. After his death, Nur ad-Din was replaced by Saladin. He was able to create a greater unity between the different Muslim groups. As you can see from the map on page 45, Saladin was able to reconquer large areas of the crusader kingdom.

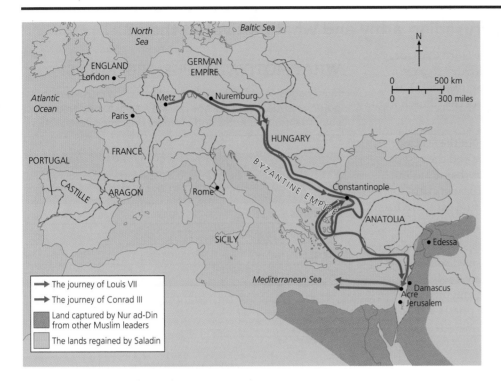

The journey of Louis VII
The journey of Conrad III
Land captured by Nur ad-Din from other Muslim leaders
The lands regained by Saladin

Stage 4: The immediate causes of the Third Crusade

Saladin led a large army of 30,000 men, including 12,000 well-trained cavalry. In 1187 he defeated the Christian army at the Battle of Hattin. Many crusaders were killed or captured. Among those captured were King Guy of Jerusalem and Reynold of Chatillon. Reynold had sunk a boat full of Muslim pilgrims travelling to Makkah (Mecca). He had also broken a truce with Saladin – attacking a caravan of Muslim traders and torturing many of the men he captured. Saladin had King Guy and Reynold sent to him. Ibn al-Athir (a contemporary Muslim historian) describes what happened next.

> He had the King seated beside him and, as he was half-dead with thirst, gave him iced water to drink. The King drank and gave the rest to Reynold, who also drank. Saladin said 'This godless man did not have my permission to drink and will not save his life that way'. He turned on Reynold and listed all his crimes and sins. Then with his own hand, he cut off the man's head. 'Twice' said Saladin, 'I have sworn to kill that man. Once when he attacked Makkah and Madinah and again when he broke the truce and attacked the caravan.'

Imad al-Din (a historian who was part of Saladin's household staff) provides a similar account, describing how Guy shook with fear because he expected to be killed as well. Guy was not killed. He seems to have been well treated and was later released after a ransom had been paid. However, Saladin did order the execution of all the Knights Templar and Knights Hospitaller – soldier priests who were sworn enemies of Saladin. Other prisoners were ransomed or sold as slaves. A few months later Saladin re-captured Jerusalem. The Muslims took Christian crosses down from the mosques but there was no other looting or destruction of the city.

The news that Saladin had captured Jerusalem spread quickly to Europe, where people were shocked and dismayed to hear that the holy city had been taken. In October 1187, Pope Gregory VIII called for a new crusade to the Holy Land. He issued a papal bull which described the horrors of the Battle of Hattin and detailed atrocities committed by Muslims. There was a great deal of enthusiasm and popular support for the crusade in England. Shock at the loss of Jerusalem quickly turned into determination to win it back and thousands of men from the countryside and the major towns rushed to join the crusade.

WHY DID SO MANY PEOPLE JOIN THE THIRD CRUSADE?

Why do you think so many people in England were willing to risk their lives and join a Third Crusade to fight against Saladin and win back Jerusalem? You will study this question in more detail on pages 46–47 but, before you do, you should form a hypothesis. Look at the list of possible reasons below. Place them in order, starting with the reason you find the most convincing and ending with the explanation you find the least credible.

- They thought that Saladin could be easily defeated.
- They thought it was their religious duty.
- They wanted to gain revenge for the Christians killed by Saladin.
- They saw it as an opportunity for a great adventure.
- They wanted to prove themselves as a great soldier or knight and win glory and honour for their family.
- They saw it as a chance to get rich.

Who joined the English crusading army and what motivated them?

Richard became famous for leading the Third Crusade, but thousands of English people also decided to go. A crusader was someone who, with the approval of his local priest, swore a vow to fight the enemies of the Church in the Holy Land.

The crusade attracted large numbers from the leading noble families. Crusading was expensive and the cost of travelling to the Holy Land by sea meant that it was out of the reach of ordinary people. Most crusaders paid for themselves; only well-trained soldiers could expect to be paid to join the crusade.

Many English knights joined the crusade, so Richard's army was made up of experienced and well-armed soldiers. Only two bishops joined the crusade, but many English priests sailed with Richard's army. They prayed and provided encouragement for the crusaders. Some priests also took an active role in key battles.

Motives: The 4 Rs

Now you have formed a hypothesis about why so many people joined the Third Crusade it is time to carry out more detailed research and to test that hypothesis. Four key reasons have been identified by historians. These can be summarised as the 4Rs – rewards, revenge, respect and religion.

WHAT MOTIVATED THE CRUSADERS?

Read pages 46–47 about what motivated the crusaders to go on crusade. Use the Knowledge Organiser below to help you organise your notes and evaluate how important each motive was.

Motives – The 4Rs	Explanation – Why did this motivate people?	Evaluation – How important was this motive?
Rewards		
Revenge		
Respect		
Religion		

1 REWARDS

The financial rewards offered to people who joined the crusade were considerable. Successful soldiers could expect to share in the 'spoils of victory' – seizing the possessions and valuables of the enemy after a battle, or capturing a town. The crusades offered a chance to have an adventure and make money.

For others, the crusade offered a chance to escape repaying debts. Crusaders were told that their family would be protected and that repayment of any debts they had would be postponed until they returned.

Another reason why there was a great rush to take the cross and join the crusade was to avoid having to pay the crusading tax. The crusade required great organisation as well as enthusiasm. This included the arrangements for collection of a crusading tax (known as the Saladin Tithe) to pay for Richard's transportation to the Holy Land and to help meet the costs of raising and supplying an enormous army. Crusaders did not have to pay this tax.

2 REVENGE

Many people were shocked at the loss of Jerusalem and the defeat of the Christian army. Propaganda played on their emotions and increased anger and the desire for revenge. Rumours circulated that Saladin's forces had pulled down the cross on the church at the hospital in Jerusalem and dragged it through the city dung heap. Paintings were produced showing Muslim knights trampling over tombs and allowing their horses to urinate over them. Though none of these events were true, the pictures were carried around by priests to persuade people to join the crusade.

3 RESPECT

For many young knights, the crusades represented an opportunity to make a name for themselves and to bring honour to their family. Soldiers and knights that were successful earned respect from their local community as well as financial rewards.

4 RELIGION

The importance of religion was at the heart of understanding why people, including Richard himself, joined the Third Crusade. Joining a crusade was a religious act as well as a great military adventure. What every Christian wanted was a full indulgence – a promise of complete forgiveness so that a person's soul could pass straight to heaven without having to go through purgatory (see page 23). In 1095 Pope Urban II promised, as God's representative on Earth, that going on crusade and fighting in a war against enemies against the Church would bring a full indulgence.

As you can see in the extract below, churchmen made similar promises in the twelfth century:

> O mighty soldier, O man of war, at last you have a cause for which you can fight without endangering your soul; a cause in which to win is glorious and for which to die is but gain … I can offer you a bargain which you cannot afford to miss. Take the sign of the cross … The cross is cheap and if you wear it with humility you will find that you obtain the Kingdom of Heaven.

Religious reasons also explain why Jerusalem was so important to people living at the time and why crusaders were so keen to fight to regain control of the city.

The religious importance of Jerusalem

◀ If you look carefully at the medieval Christian map, you will see that Jerusalem is at the centre of the world. Christians believed that Jerusalem was the holiest place on God's Earth. It was the place where Jesus was crucified and rose again. In the fourth century, the Roman Emperor Constantine announced that Christians could worship freely. His mother, Helena, was a Christian and ordered the building of the Church of the Holy Sepulchre on the site of the crucifixion. Christians called the area around Jerusalem 'the Holy Land' because it was where Jesus had lived. During the eleventh and twelfth centuries more and more Christians travelled to Jerusalem, as this was seen as the most sacred site to go to on a **pilgrimage**. The main aim of the Third Crusade was therefore to recapture Jerusalem from Muslim control.

4.3 Communicating your answer: Thinking about causation (part 2)

In your exam you will be asked to explain why events occurred.

Look at the practice question below:

Explain why people from England joined the Third Crusade. (12 marks)

This 'explain' question focuses on the key historical concept of causation. Remember to use what you have already learnt about answering 'explain' questions that focus on causation.

Use the advice on this page to answer the practice question above. Make sure you use your Knowledge Organiser from page 46 to help you.

THINK BACK AND CONNECT

Look again at the advice provided on page 26 about answering causation questions:

- Cover a range of factors/causes – do not spend your whole answer on one cause.
- Organise your answer using categories. For the question above you could use the 4Rs (see pages 46–47). Remember to start a new paragraph for each factor.
- Prioritise the causes. Which factors were the most important? Some causes/factors are likely to be more important than others. Historians enjoy arguing about the relative importance of different causes.
- Explain why you think some causes were more important than others. Prove your claim.

You can use the acronym ROPE (Range–Organise–Prioritise–Explain) to help you remember these key points.

Prioritising causes: Mind your language!

You need to be careful with the language you use when you write about different causes. Select words and phrases very carefully – aim to be as precise as possible – so that your argument about which causes are the most important is very clear to your reader. You can use the word wall below to help you find the right language to express your arguments clearly.

Practice question

Use page 49 to make notes on Richard's motives for joining the Third Crusade. Talk through with a partner and plan how you would answer this 12-mark practice question that also focuses on the concept of causation:

Explain why Richard I joined the Third Crusade.

If you want to show that a factor was the most important cause	If you want to show that a cause was very important	If you want to show a cause was important
… was the essential reason why …	A crucial reason why … was …	… also played an important role in …
… was the main cause of …	… played a major role in …	… influenced …
The key reason for … was …	… was a significant reason for …	… contributed to …
The most influential reason for … was …	… was also highly important in …	… also determined why …

What were Richard's motives for involvement in the Third Crusade?

In the autumn of 1187, after the news of Saladin's conquests in the Holy Land, Richard agreed to go on crusade. He was the first prince to announce that he was going and he acted without his father's permission. Richard was genuinely committed to going on crusade. A crusade was a religious act as well as a great military adventure. The Holy Land was the emotional centre of the Christian world. Richard also had a personal connection to the Holy Land – he was the great grandson of Fulk of Anjou, King of Jerusalem from 1134–42.

Richard was also a soldier and no war could bring greater prestige or honour. Richard may also have seen the crusade as an opportunity to make a name for himself and to be remembered as a great warrior.

The Third Crusade was led by the three most powerful men in Europe. Richard I was joined by the King of France, Philip II and Frederick I, King of Germany (see below). This must have given Richard added confidence that the Third Crusade would be successful.

Frederick I was the most experienced of the three leaders. He had been Emperor of Germany for 36 years. Frederick was also known as 'Barbarossa', meaning 'red beard'. He had brought the barons of Germany under control and ruled over a vast area of land. This made him more wealthy and powerful than either Richard or Philip. Frederick had taken part in the Second Crusade and now, in his late sixties, he was setting out for the Holy Land again. He led a large and well-equipped army.

Richard I was confident in his own military ability and the resources he had at his disposal. He already had a great deal of military experience from his time as Duke of Aquitaine (see page 32). Thanks to the wealth that came from the Angevin Empire, he also had enormous resources with which to fight with. He introduced a special tax to pay for the crusade, known as the Saladin Tithe. He also sold vast amounts of land and property in order to raise money for his army (see page 39). All of this meant that Richard set out on crusade in 1190 with a large and very well-resourced army.

Philip II was a strong and experienced leader who had already ruled France for ten years. Philip was reluctant to join the crusade as he was worried his absence might weaken his control over the French kingdom. However, Philip, like many of the great men of Europe, was swept along by the tide of public opinion. In France, preachers stirred up enthusiasm and men who did not take the cross received gifts of distaff and wool, implying they were no better than women. Richard was Philip's vassal for the Angevin lands he held in France (Normandy, Anjou and Aquitaine). Philip's army was smaller and not as well equipped as Richard's. This angered Philip and added to the personal rivalry that already existed between the two kings.

THINKING ABOUT THE DECISIONS THAT PEOPLE TOOK IN THE PAST

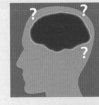

On the pages that follow you will explore what happened on the Third Crusade. Richard faced many difficult decisions. To help you understand and remember these decisions better, we will be asking you to step into Richard's shoes and make some of those difficult decisions yourself.

Your challenge starts now.

- How would you travel to the Holy Land? By foot or by ship? (Look at what happened to those who travelled on foot to the Second Crusade – see page 44.)
- Would you leave before, after or at the same time as Philip?
- How would you divide up any valuables you gain on crusade? Would you share them with the other leaders (Frederick I and Philip II)?

4.4 Why did Richard fail to recapture Jerusalem?

The main aim of the Third Crusade was to recapture Jerusalem from Saladin. The crusaders won some important battles and twice came within a few miles of the holy city, but ultimately they failed to take Jerusalem. Why was this? Was Richard's leadership a crucial factor in the failure?

THE THIRD CRUSADE: PART 1

As you explore what happened on the Third Crusade (pages 50–57) use the Knowledge Organiser below to record evidence that will help you explain why Richard failed to recapture Jerusalem. Start by using the information on this page.

Richard's leadership		Evidence that other factors caused problems for the crusaders
Evidence that Richard showed great leadership	Evidence that Richard made mistakes	

Frederick's journey to the Holy Land

1 Frederick sets off

May 1189: Frederick decided to travel by land, leading his forces through Hungary and then the **Byzantine Empire**.

2 Frederick faces problems in Anatolia

April 1190: Frederick entered the territory of the Seljuk Turks who ambushed the German army. Frederick's army also suffered from hunger and thirst. In May, the German army reached the Seljuk capital of Iconium. They managed to capture the city before continuing south towards Armenia.

3 Disaster strikes

June 1190: Frederick had almost reached the Holy Land when he drowned trying to cross a river. With their leader dead, many German knights headed home. This seriously weakened the crusaders. Some of Frederick's army continued to Acre but the loss of Frederick and so many men was a terrible blow to the Third Crusade.

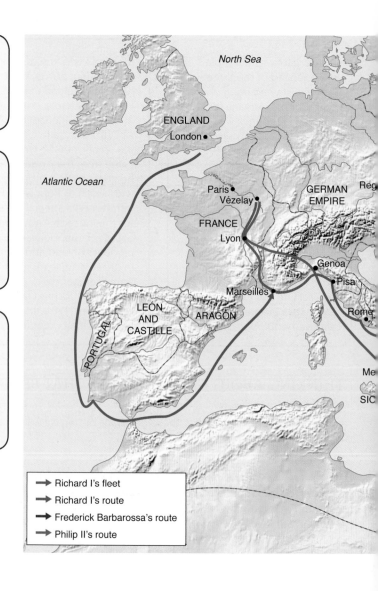

→ Richard I's fleet
→ Richard I's route
→ Frederick Barbarossa's route
→ Philip II's route

Richard's journey to the Holy Land

1 Richard's first decisions

- Richard decided to travel to the Holy Land by sea. Building and hiring ships was very expensive but travelling by sea would be quicker and safer.
- Richard made sure his army was very well disciplined. Strict punishments were introduced for anyone who caused problems on the ships. A crusader who attacked someone with a knife would have his hands chopped off.
- Richard did not trust Philip so there was a delay in setting off until both kings agreed to leave at the same time.
- The two kings made an important agreement – they were going to share the land that they won, the money they gained and the glory equally.
- Richard and Philip set out from Vézelay on 4 July 1190. At Lyon their armies divided but they agreed to meet in Sicily.

2 Sicily

September 1190: Richard entered Messina, the capital of Sicily, with trumpets and a great display. Philip had arrived quietly the week before.

The crusaders and the mainly Greek population of Messina took a violent dislike to each other and in October 1190 fighting broke out. Richard decided to settle the matter by force and seized control of Messina. Philip refused to help and was annoyed when Richard's banners were placed over the city walls as a display of triumph. Richard eventually agreed to take his banners down and give Philip one third of the money he had made from a peace deal with Tancred, the ruler of Sicily.

In April 1191, Richard's huge fleet (numbering over 200 ships and around 17,000 soldiers) left Sicily.

3 The conquest of Cyprus

On the third day after leaving Messina there was a bad storm. Most of Richard's fleet safely reached the coast of Cyprus, but three ships were driven aground and had their cargo stolen. The ruler of Cyprus (Isaac) refused to co-operate with Richard.

Richard decided to invade the island. Richard landed at Limassol, storming the shore and taking the city. Isaac eventually surrendered on 1 June 1190. Richard's conquest of Cyprus was a major achievement. The mountains made it difficult, but Richard's campaign was very well planned and carefully carried out. Cyprus was of great strategic importance as it provided a crucial link between mainland Europe and the Holy Land.

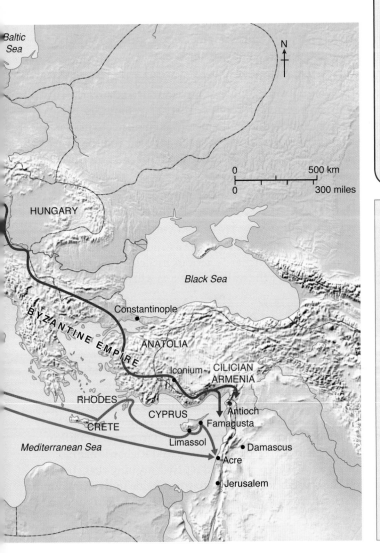

DECISION TIME

While sailing to the Holy Land from Cyprus, Richard would have been aware that he had to make some important decisions. Read the situations below. What would you do?

- **Decision 1:** Philip has now arrived in the Holy Land (at Acre). He is demanding half of everything you have taken from Cyprus. Would you agree to share with Philip?
- **Decision 2:** There are disagreements over who should be the King of Jerusalem. Philip wants to replace Guy of Lusignan (who had been king when Saladin captured Jerusalem) with his ally, Conrad of Montferrat (who had bravely defended the town of Tyre against an attack from Saladin). Guy has been to Cyprus to ask for Richard's support. Would you support him or Conrad?
- **Decision 3:** At Acre, the crusaders (including Philip) are laying siege to the town. Would you join them or plan your own attack?
- **Decision 4:** If you manage to capture Acre what would you do with any prisoners you take?

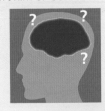

THE THIRD CRUSADE: PART 2

1 Use the information on pages 52–53 to continue to fill in your Knowledge Organiser from page 50. Remember to look for signs of good or bad leadership from Richard and to record any factors that explain why the Third Crusade did not succeed.

2 Discuss with a partner: How far does Richard deserve the credit for the crusaders military victory at Acre?

Military victory at Acre

The crusaders were already laying siege to Acre when Philip and then Richard arrived in the Holy Land. Acre had fallen to Saladin in July 1187. It was the largest town and the main port in the Kingdom of Jerusalem (see map on page 44). Baha al-Din Qaragush (one of Saladin's most experienced commanders) was in charge of defending the city. Philip reached Acre in January 1191. He was content to join the siege and he continued the work of bombarding the walls of the town.

Richard was sailing towards Acre on 7 June 1191 when he saw a huge ship coming from Beirut weighed down with supplies and reinforcements for Saladin's army at Acre. Richard's ships moved close to the great ship and, after a fierce and long struggle, were able to sink it. When Richard arrived at Acre on 8 June, he was given a hero's welcome. He had conquered Cyprus, which meant that the crusading army had a secure supply line from Europe, and he had sunk one of the enemy's main ships. He also brought with him a vast amount of equipment and supplies. All of this was an important psychological boost to the Christian army.

Gradually, the bombardment of Acre was increased as Richard brought up his siege machines to join those already set up by Philip. Slowly but surely the walls of Acre were battered down.

An important breakthrough came when Philip's miners were able to tunnel under and collapse a section of the wall protecting Acre. However, a French attack was beaten back by the garrison defending the city. By this point, Saladin's garrison was exhausted. They were getting little or no sleep as their relatively small numbers meant they had to remain permanently at arms. In contrast, the crusaders had enough men to regularly swap their assault troops, allowing some rest while fresh men took their place.

On 11 July Richard's forces attacked, coming very close to success. It was at this point that the defenders decided it was time to give up. On 12 July the garrison surrendered the city and all it contained to the crusaders. This included stores, artillery and ships. The capture of Saladin's fleet was important as it meant that he could no longer challenge crusader dominance at sea. It was agreed that the lives of those within the garrison and their wives and children would be spared in return for a ransom. Richard and Philip's banners were raised above the walls of the devastated city.

Richard's quarrel with Philip

By this point Philip was thinking of returning home. There were a number of reasons for this. Philip was jealous of Richard's successes in Sicily and Cyprus and the two kings had a number of quarrels. Philip had been angered by Richard's actions in Sicily, especially when Richard had arrogantly placed his banners over the walls of Messina when both kings were in the capital.

When they arrived in the Holy Land, Richard and Philip often competed against each other for knights who would join their service. Philip offered to pay three gold pieces to any knight who would join him, but Richard, who offered four gold pieces, often outbid him. In addition, the two kings argued over who should be the King of Jerusalem (Philip was allied to Conrad of Montferrat while Richard supported Guy of Lusignan).

However, perhaps Philip's main reason for abandoning the crusade was the death of the Count of Flanders at Acre. Philip saw an opportunity to take control of the rich lands the Count controlled in Artois, which bordered France. Richard tried to persuade Philip to remain in the Holy Land until Jerusalem was recovered. Philip told Richard that he would only stay if Richard gave him half of Cyprus. Richard refused, arguing that their agreement to share gains made on the crusade only related to gains made in the Kingdom of Jerusalem. On 3 August Philip set sail for home. Philip left Duke Hugh of Burgundy as commander of the French forces.

Richard's treatment of prisoners

It was now up to Richard to make sure that Saladin kept to the peace terms that had been agreed. Negotiations continued until 20 August. Saladin seemed to be in no hurry to pay the ransom money. Rumours started to spread that Saladin had killed the crusaders he had taken as prisoner. The crusaders feared that Saladin would deliberately use the negotiations as a delaying tactic. If he was going to capture Jerusalem, Richard needed to move on from Acre. However, he could not afford to march away leaving only a small number of men to guard nearly 3,000 enemy soldiers. Even to feed so many men would be difficult since, on Saladin's order, the countryside around Acre had been devastated. To free the prisoners, without the full ransom being paid, would have damaged the confidence of the crusaders in Richard's leadership. Also, once free, the prisoners might re-join Saladin's army. The diagram opposite summarises Richard's problems.

Saladin's failure to pay the ransom within the agreed time limit therefore placed Richard in a difficult position. The decision he took, after consulting with other leaders, is highly controversial and has been heavily criticised by modern historians (see page 42). On 20 August, Richard's men marched more than 2,600 prisoners out of the city to an area of open ground beyond the crusaders' tents. It was here that they were massacred with swords in cold blood.

I need to move on – Saladin is using negotiations over the prisoners to slow me down.

I need all my soldiers – I cannot afford to leave some behind to guard the prisoners.

How am I going to feed the prisoners?

What will my men think of me if I free the prisoners?

If I let the prisoners go, they will re-join Saladin's army.

▲ A French painting from 1490 showing Richard watching the execution of Muslim prisoners.

DECISION TIME

Richard now prepared his troops for an 80-mile march, in intense heat, along the coast to Jaffa (an important port, from which the crusaders planned to launch an attack on Jerusalem). He knew that this would be a dangerous march as his army would be at risk from attack from Saladin's mounted archers. It was important that Richard decided on the right formation for his army.

1 How would you have organised the crusaders for the march to Jaffa?

2 Draw a plan showing where you would position the following:
   a) Mounted knights (your key attacking weapon – the knights and their horses needed to be protected until the moment to charge came)
   b) Infantry (well-armed soldiers who fought on foot)
   c) Archers
   d) The baggage train (this was pulled by horses and carried important supplies and valuables).

3 How would you use your navy?

4 What instructions would you give your army?
   a) Stay together at all times – do not chase after the enemy; or
   b) Take the opportunity to charge at the enemy if you see an opportunity.

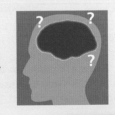

THE THIRD CRUSADE: PART 3

Use the information on pages 54–55 to continue to fill in your Knowledge Organiser from page 50. Remember to look for signs of good or bad leadership from Richard and to record any factors that explain why the Third Crusade did not succeed.

Discuss with a partner: How far does Richard deserve the credit for the crusader's military victory at the Battle of Arsuf?

The march to Jaffa

On 25 August, the dangerous march to Jaffa began. Richard left Acre with approximately 15,000 troops. At Acre, the crusaders had found themselves in a siege situation that they were familiar with. They had been protected from the highly skilled Turkish cavalry. However, on the road to Jaffa, Richard had to think carefully about how to protect his men, as they would be at constant risk from attacks led by Saladin's mounted archers. The weapons of the Turkish cavalry were lighter than those of the crusaders. In hand-to-hand fighting, the crusaders held the advantage but the speed and agility of the Turkish cavalry meant that they were very effective at attacking an enemy on the move.

The march to Jaffa was an excellent demonstration of effective tactics. Richard ordered the crusaders to march close to the seashore, their right flank protected by the sea and by their fleet. The capture of Saladin's fleet at Acre meant that there was no danger of an attack from the sea.

The chief tactical weapon of the crusaders was the charge of their heavily armoured knights. The knights and their horses had to be protected until the moment to charge came. Richard gave the job of protecting them to spearmen and archers who were trained to draw up a defensive screen, surrounding the knights like a wall and forcing the Turks to stay out of range. As these foot soldiers had to fight off the constant Turkish attacks, Richard divided them into two groups who took it in turns to protect the left flank. One half would protect the crusaders against attack while the other half took things easy marching beside the baggage train between the knights and the sea. Richard's military leadership was crucial – he kept tight control of his troops, making sure that no crusader would break rank to give chase to Saladin's cavalry. He knew that it would make his army vulnerable to attack if they broke formation.

While the crusaders were marching towards Jaffa, Saladin marched south on a parallel course. He kept the main body of his troops at a safe distance from the crusaders, but he frequently sent in small bands of men to attack Richard's left flank. Saladin's men made the march even more difficult by advancing ahead of the crusading army and destroying fortresses and burning crops. This meant food was scarce and there was nowhere to rest in safety. The heat was intense – made worse by the heavy armour that the crusaders wore. Sunstroke claimed many victims. However, the presence of the fleet enabled Richard to keep his men supplied and he was able to provide rest and treatment aboard his ships for those troops that were sick or exhausted.

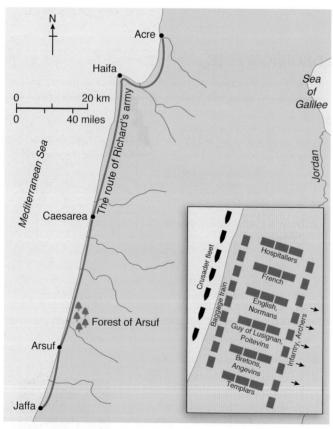

▲ The march to Jaffa. The inset shows the formation of Richard's army on the march. How similar is it to the formation you chose?

The Battle of Arsuf

By early September, Saladin realised that the tactics he was using were not going to stop the crusaders. If he had any hope of stopping their advance, he had to commit to a major battle. Saladin picked his battleground – the plain to the north of Arsuf. During the mid-morning of 7 September, Saladin made his move, ordering his force of 30,000 men to attack the crusaders as they emerged from the wooded hills onto the plain. Turkish horseman charged at the crusaders and launched a rain of arrows so thick that crusaders commented that even the bright sunlight was dimmed. The crusaders started to lose horses at an alarming rate, and were struggling in the intense heat.

Eventually, two knights in the rear guard lost their patience and charged at the enemy. Dangerously, many knights started to gallop after them, breaking the infantry screen that protected the crusaders. This was the critical moment in the battle. The crusader counter attack had to be supported before the superior numbers of the Turks overwhelmed them. Without hesitation, Richard and his own knights joined the charge, ordering other knights to do the same. There was a fierce struggle with both sides throwing more and more men into the fray, but eventually a series of charges led by Richard and William des Barres forced Saladin to withdraw. Richard's southward march could continue. Three days later, on 10 September, the crusader army reached Jaffa.

DECISION TIME

Richard now faced another important decision. Jaffa was an important port and it provided a good base from which to launch an attack on Jerusalem. However, Saladin had destroyed the city's walls and fortifications. If the crusaders wanted to use Jaffa as a strong base the walls needed to be rebuilt.

Jaffa was also the ideal point from which to launch an attack on Ascalon. This city had an impressive harbour, through which supplies could be brought in, and its fortress guarded the road that linked Egypt and Syria. The capture of Ascalon would cut off Saladin's military and trade links with Egypt.

What would you do next?
- a) Attack Jerusalem straight away.
- b) Rebuild the fortifications at Jaffa.
- c) Attack Ascalon straight away.

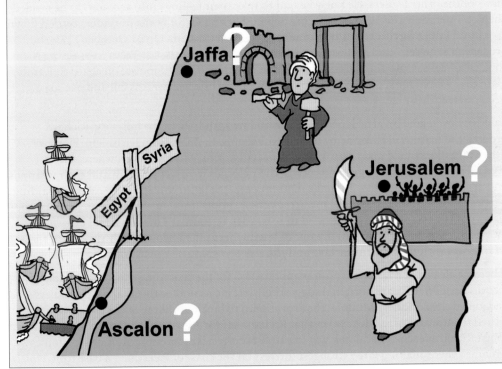

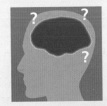

THE THIRD CRUSADE: PART 4

Use the information on pages 56–57 to continue to fill in your Knowledge Organiser from page 50. Remember to look for signs of good or bad leadership from Richard and to record any factors that explain why the Third Crusade did not succeed.

Discuss with a partner: How far should Richard be blamed for his decision not to attack Jerusalem in July 1192?

The first attempt to take Jerusalem, October 1191–January 1192

Richard argued against launching an attack on Jerusalem for two main reasons:

> We do not have enough troops to lay siege to Jerusalem and protect our supply line. During the march from Acre to Jaffa, our navy could support us from the sea. If we march on Jerusalem, the Turkish army could cut our supply lines.

> Even if we do take Jerusalem, we need more resources, more money and more people to settle and defend both the city and the coastal towns we have taken.

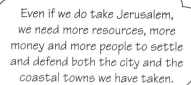

Richard argued for going straight to Ascalon, but the majority of the crusaders (including the French and German troops who remained in the Holy Land) preferred to stay and re-fortify Jaffa, before launching an attack on Jerusalem. Reluctantly, Richard gave way to the views of the other leaders. He knew he had to take their feelings into account, as he needed their co-operation and support. During September and October the crusaders settled down to rebuild Jaffa's fortifications before advancing on Jerusalem. On 31 October 1191, the crusading army left Jaffa and occupied the two ruined fortresses at Yasur; rebuilding them took two weeks. Once the fortresses had been repaired, Richard moved on again to Ramla. Here they waited for six weeks, stockpiling supplies while heavy rains fell and the road became steadily worse.

Saladin now feared an attack on Jerusalem and he withdrew to the holy city. Richard ordered the main crusading army to Beit Nuba, only 12 miles from Jerusalem. However, heavy rains continued and there were violent hailstorms. Mud was everywhere, the crusaders' food became soggy and rotten, their clothes were wet through and their weapons and armour started to rust. To make matters worse, Saladin continued to send out raiding parties to ambush the crusaders and attack their supply lines. At a meeting in January, the leaders of the crusading army decided to turn back to Ramla. This was a real blow to the morale of the soldiers, who still dreamt of 'saving' Jerusalem. However, by this point the weather conditions were unbearable and the risk too great.

It became clear that a far better military option was for the crusading army to take and rebuild Ascalon (Richard's original suggestion), but it was not for this that many soldiers had joined the crusade. At Ramla, the army began to break up. Some of the French soldiers retired to Jaffa and Acre. This meant that Richard left for Ascalon with a much smaller army. When Richard reached Ascalon it was in ruins. For the next four months, Richard's forces remained there, making it the strongest fortress on the coast of Palestine – a base from which Richard could attack Saladin's forces as they travelled between Egypt and Syria.

The second attempt to take Jerusalem, June–July 1192

In May 1192, Richard attacked the fortress of Darum. Its capture added to the length of the coastline in the hands of the crusaders (see map). During this time the other crusader leaders met and decided that they would attack Jerusalem for the second time. When Richard returned from Darum they advanced once more on Jerusalem. Benefiting from better weather and a weakened opponent, it took the crusaders five days to advance to Beit Nuba, a journey that the previous year had taken them two months. Saladin ordered that all the wells around Jerusalem should be poisoned and, fearing an attack, he prepared to leave the city.

Meanwhile, there was fierce debate in the crusader camp about what to do next. Richard argued that the vulnerability of the supply line back to Jaffa, the lack of water and Jerusalem's formidable defences made it highly unlikely that any attack would be successful. The remaining French troops wanted to continue, but Richard decided to turn back.

Richard has been criticised for this decision. Some historians argue that Saladin was in such difficulties in Jerusalem that the city could have been retaken. Saladin's financial resources were becoming overstretched and he was struggling to pay for the ongoing war. However, Richard did not know that Saladin was in a desperate position and, even if the city could have been taken, it is unlikely that it could have been retained for long. At some point many of the crusaders would want to go home, their pilgrimage completed, their vows fulfilled. It was unlikely that the majority could be persuaded to live in Jerusalem and defend it.

In addition, Richard had heard worrying news from back home – John and Philip were plotting against him. Richard was therefore keen to negotiate a peace settlement with Saladin and return home as quickly as possible. However, on 27 July Saladin launched a surprise attack on Jaffa. His troops were able to bring down a large section of the defensive wall of the city, and the garrison defending Jaffa offered to surrender. Richard arrived at Jaffa just in time. Despite knowing that his men would be heavily outnumbered, Richard launched an immediate attack. The surprise attack worked to Richard's advantage and Saladin was forced to withdraw. This was a crucial victory. The crusaders' lands would have been cut into two separate parts if Saladin had been successful and captured Jaffa.

Richard's victory at Jaffa demonstrated his skill and bravery as a military leader. It also demonstrated to Saladin that he could not drive the crusaders out of the Holy Land. Negotiation was now the only option. At the end of August, Saladin proposed peace terms in the form of the Treaty of Jaffa.

In the month after the Treaty of Jaffa was signed, groups of crusaders made their way to Jerusalem. Richard did not go to the holy city. Perhaps he was too ill, or perhaps he could not bear to see the city still in the hands of Saladin. On 9 October 1192, Richard set sail for home. The Third Crusade was over.

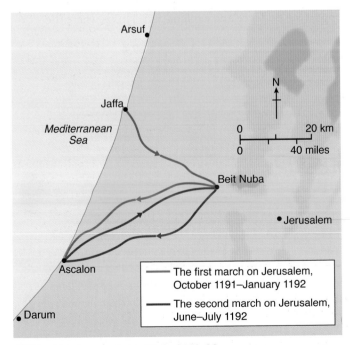

▲ The marches on Jerusalem, 1191-92.

THE TREATY OF JAFFA

- Saladin was to retain control of Jerusalem.
- The crusaders were allowed to keep their conquests of Acre and Jaffa and the coastal strip between the two towns.
- Muslims and Christians were granted free passage through each other's lands.
- Christian pilgrims were allowed access to the Church of the Holy Sepulchre in Jerusalem.

4.5 Communicating your answer: Thinking about causation (part 3)

By now you should have built up a good understanding of the Third Crusade. Remember that the main aim of the crusade was to recapture Jerusalem. You should feel confident about answering this practice question:

Explain why Richard and his fellow crusaders failed to recapture Jerusalem. (12 marks)

On page 48 we saw how the acronym ROPE (Range-Organise-Prioritise-Explain) can help you remember the key steps you need to take for this type of question.

Step 1: List a **range** of reasons why Richard failed to recapture Jerusalem. Use your Knowledge Organiser from page 50 to help you.

Step 2: Organise your answer. You could sort your reasons into the categories below but you may want to follow your own plan.

Reasons for Richard's failure to recapture Jerusalem

- **Richard's leadership:** Did Richard make mistakes? Should he have continued on to Jerusalem? Was he to blame for Philip's departure home? Or did Richard show skilful and brave leadership? Does he deserve credit for the successes the crusading army had? Did he achieve as much as was possible?
- **Weaknesses within the crusading army:** How damaging was Frederick's death? Was disunity the main factor that weakened the crusading army?
- **The strength of the opposition:** Could anyone have defeated Saladin's well-led, large, united and well-motivated army? Was Saladin in too strong a position to be defeated? Did the crusaders face an impossible task, as they would not have been able to hold on to Jerusalem in the longer term, even if an attack had been successful?

Step 3: Prioritise the causes. The word wall on page 48 will help you find the right language to express your arguments. This is where the debates start! What was the key factor?

Step 4: Make sure you **explain** and support your arguments. Historians have to justify their arguments by providing supporting evidence and explanation. This is where the images of a rope and bridge comes in useful!

Visible learning

Using connectives to tie what you know to the question

When talking or writing about a cause or factor, you cannot simply say that it was important. You have to prove that it was. You can do this by using some of the golden words and phrases highlighted in the example here, such as 'this meant that', 'this led to' and 'this resulted in'. These phrases are called connectives because they tie what you know to the question and help you prove your argument.

Frederick's death on his journey to the Holy Land weakened the crusaders. It resulted in the loss of an experienced leader and meant that many of his men decided to return home. This reduced the size of the crusading army. Richard's arrogance and actions on the crusade caused problems. His failure to share the gains made from the conquest of Cyprus angered Philip, as did quarrels over who should be the next King of Jerusalem. This contributed to the French King returning home.

Visible learning

How does talking and debating help?

Students usually write better answers if they have first talked through their answer with other people. Talking helps us organise ideas in our mind, choose the right words and decide what evidence we need to prove our points. Debating helps us test our arguments and decide if we have enough evidence to support our key points. Think of your overall argument as being a bridge that needs supporting pillars and strong foundations. If the pillars are not strong – the bridge crumbles.

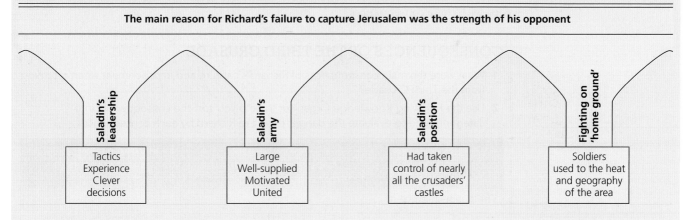

The main reason for Richard's failure to capture Jerusalem was the strength of his opponent

Saladin's leadership — Tactics, Experience, Clever decisions

Saladin's army — Large, Well-supplied, Motivated, United

Saladin's position — Had taken control of nearly all the crusaders' castles

Fighting on 'home ground' — Soldiers used to the heat and geography of the area

DECISION TIME

Hopefully placing yourselves in the position of Richard at key times during the Third Crusade made you realise the difficulties he faced. Even returning home proved to be difficult. Use the map below to try and plan a safe route home. What route would you have taken given the dangers highlighted on the map? Remember:

- Richard needed to get home as quickly as possible as John was causing problems in England and Philip was threatening his lands in Normandy.
- Winter was closing in and the longer he stayed at sea, the greater the risk of shipwreck.
- The time of year meant it was too dangerous to sail to England or France via the Atlantic.

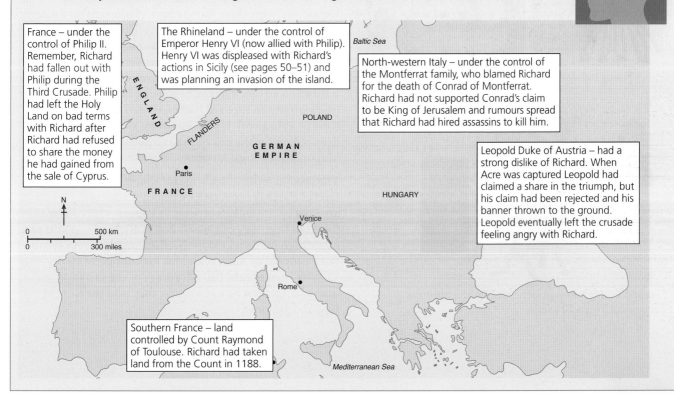

France – under the control of Philip II. Remember, Richard had fallen out with Philip during the Third Crusade. Philip had left the Holy Land on bad terms with Richard after Richard had refused to share the money he had gained from the sale of Cyprus.

The Rhineland – under the control of Emperor Henry VI (now allied with Philip). Henry VI was displeased with Richard's actions in Sicily (see pages 50–51) and was planning an invasion of the island.

North-western Italy – under the control of the Montferrat family, who blamed Richard for the death of Conrad of Montferrat. Richard had not supported Conrad's claim to be King of Jerusalem and rumours spread that Richard had hired assassins to kill him.

Leopold Duke of Austria – had a strong dislike of Richard. When Acre was captured Leopold had claimed a share in the triumph, but his claim had been rejected and his banner thrown to the ground. Leopold eventually left the crusade feeling angry with Richard.

Southern France – land controlled by Count Raymond of Toulouse. Richard had taken land from the Count in 1188.

4.6 What were the consequences of the Third Crusade?

The story of the Third Crusade does not end with the Treaty of Jaffa. Just as dramatic was its aftermath and what happened when Richard tried to return from the Holy Land. His capture and the lengthy time he spent imprisoned gave John and Phillip the opportunity to plot against him and attack his lands. The enormous ransom that had to be paid for his release from captivity placed a massive financial burden on England. How did Richard cope with these consequences?

CONSEQUENCES OF THE THIRD CRUSADE

1 What were the main consequences of Richard's capture and imprisonment when returning from the Third Crusade?

2 Use the following Knowledge Organiser to help you sort the consequences into categories and to evaluate the danger posed to Richard by each consequence.

Factor	Explain – What were the consequences?	Evaluation – How dangerous was this to Richard?
The financial burden		
Threat to Richard's lands in England		
Threat to Richard's lands in France		

▲ Richard being taken prisoner in Vienna after his unsuccessful Third Crusade.

Richard's capture

Richard's aim was probably to head for the land of his brother-in-law, Henry the Lion, in the north east of Germany. To get there he may have planned to go through the territory of the king of Hungary. However, stormy weather meant that as he sailed back to Europe, he landed further west than he intended (near Venice). Richard knew that he had landed in a very dangerous location. Northern Italy was controlled by the nephew of Conrad of Monferrat (the man whom Richard had prevented from becoming King of Jerusalem). It was important that Richard was not detected, so for the rest of the journey Richard took with him only a few loyal knights.

The need to move quickly meant that Richard entered the land of the Duke of Austria without realising it. He was arrested by the Duke's officers in Vienna, where he was found hiding in a poor man's house. Richard was sent to a castle high on a rocky slope overlooking the river Danube. Both Leopold of Austria and his lord, Emperor Henry VI, were keen to take full advantage of the situation and immediately let it be known that they held the King of England prisoner.

John causes problems

In the meantime, Richard's brother, John, saw an opportunity to seize control of the Angevin Empire and become king. In January 1193, he travelled to Philip II's court in Paris where he paid homage to the French King for Normandy and Richard's other lands in France. John promised to marry Philip's sister (Alice) and to hand over the Norman Vexin (land on the border between France and Normandy) to Philip. John then returned to England to stir up rebellion. He asked for help from William, King of the Scots, but this was refused. John gathered together some Welsh and Flemish mercenaries and used them to take over the castles of Windsor and Wallingford. He then claimed the kingdom for himself, saying that his brother was dead.

Richard's ransom and its burden on England

Only a few barons believed John and he gained very few supporters and very little territory. Walter of Coutances (the justiciar whom Richard had left in control of England) called together a meeting of the leading barons at Oxford in February. They sent messengers to Germany to find out more information. In March, Henry and Leopold agreed terms for Richard's ransom and the price was fixed at 100,000 marks. This was an enormous sum of money – more than twice Richard's annual income from the whole of England. In England, a 25 per cent tax on income and the amount of moveable property each individual owned (known as 'an aid') was introduced. Taxes had already been raised to pay for Richard's crusade (see page 46). Now came another massive financial demand on the entire population.

Philip causes problems in Normandy

In Normandy, Philip was attacking Richard's lands. Philip played upon fears that Richard would never be freed and this weakened the determination of lords in Normandy to resist Philip's invasion of the duchy. In April, the great frontier castle of Gisors surrendered to the King of France.

The terms of Richard's ransom were finally settled on 29 June. Richard would be freed once the emperor had received 100,000 marks. By December 1193, the money to pay Richard's ransom had been collected. John was now desperate, and in January 1194 he made a treaty with Philip. John surrendered the whole of Normandy east of the River Seine to Philip, except for the city of Rouen and the surrounding area. Philip and John approached Emperor Henry VI with an alternative bid. They offered him 150,000 marks if he would keep Richard for a whole year or hand him over to them. However, a group of German princes persuaded the emperor to reject Philip and John's offer.

Richard is released

Richard was finally released on 4 February 1194. Henry sent Philip and John a letter telling them that he would do all he could to help Richard if everything that had been taken was not restored at once. Philip ignored this threat and began to take possession of the territories that John had surrendered to him in the treaty of January 1194. He captured many strongholds in Normandy and was now within easy striking distance of Rouen, the capital city.

Richard arrived back in England in March. While Richard had been away, Philip had gained some land, but Richard's empire had not collapsed under pressure from Philip and John. The large sum raised to pay Richard's ransom shows how effectively the system of government he had left in place had functioned. However, on his return, Richard was faced with a daunting task. Philip had encouraged some of the lords of Aquitaine to rise in revolt and he himself had made important gains in Normandy. For Richard to win back this land would add to the heavy financial burdens already placed on his subjects by the King's ransom.

INTERPRETATIONS ❓

1 What does the case study of what happened at Nottingham castle tell us about Richard's character?

2 How do you think Richard's actions at Nottingham would have been viewed by his contemporaries (people living at the time)?

3 Read page 63. Why do you think contemporaries viewed Richard's actions on crusade differently to some modern historians?

4 How do you think Richard's actions on crusade should be viewed? Debate these questions:
   a) How far were his actions 'brutal and stupid'?
   b) How far did he display 'remarkable military leadership'?
   c) How far should the Third Crusade be viewed as a success?

Case Study: March 1194 – Nottingham Castle

By the time Richard returned to England, most of the castles held in John's name had already surrendered. The only two still holding out were Tickhill and Nottingham. Both of these were under siege from operations started by Hubert Walter (now Archbishop of Canterbury and Richard's justiciar). The garrison at Tickhill sent two knights to see if Richard had landed and when it was confirmed that the King was back, the castle immediately surrendered. Nottingham, however, continued to hold out.

Richard arrived in Nottingham on 25 March at the head of a large army, bringing with him siege machines, stone throwing trebuchets, carpenters and his expert engineers. Richard gave the order for an immediate assault on the castle. As usual, Richard led his army from the front, wearing only light mail and an iron cap. Heavy shields held aloft by his bodyguards protected him from the hail of arrows being fired by the defenders of the castle. The garrison defending the castle put up strong resistance, but by the end of the first day of fighting the outer battlements had fallen.

The following morning Richard sent messengers to the garrison defending the castle, ordering them to surrender to their king. At first they refused, not believing that Richard had returned. Richard brought up his siege artillery and had gallows erected in full view of those defending the castle. Some of the soldiers captured the previous day were hanged. The message was clear; if the soldiers inside continued to defend the castle, they would suffer the same fate. Soon after the garrison surrendered. Richard was now in full military control of England. In May, he left England for the Continent, determined to take back the land that Philip had taken while he was in captivity and to strengthen Normandy's defences. He never returned.

▲ Nottingham Castle, the last castle held in John's name to surrender to Richard on his return to England.

What impact did the Third Crusade have on Richard's reputation?

Richard's actions on the Third Crusade were praised by most contemporaries. Richard had fought bravely to fulfil his religious duties and, despite the failure to recapture Jerusalem, significant territorial gains had been made. People at the time accepted the need for Richard to raise large sums of money to fight costly and dangerous wars overseas. They even seemed to accept his brutal treatment of prisoners. Contemporary Christian commentators regarded the massacre at Acre (see page 53) as a consequence of Saladin's failure to keep the terms of the treaty agreed after the battle. They also point out that Richard's actions were important militarily because if the prisoners were allowed to return to Saladin's ranks, they could have gone on to do a great deal of harm to the Christian army. In addition, contemporaries believed that the coastal towns of Arsuf, Jaffa and Ascalon fell into Richard's hands because the citizens of these towns no longer trusted Saladin to help them.

It is reported that Saladin was furious with Richard for the massacre and that he later ordered that Christian prisoners should be put to death in revenge. Massacres had occurred before the Third Crusade. It is estimated that between 3,000 and 10,000 Muslims were massacred when Jerusalem was taken by the Christian army during the First Crusade (see page 43). Massacres had also been carried out by Muslims, for example, by Turks when they captured land from Christians in the East before the First Crusade, by Zengi at Edessa in 1144 and by Saladin in taking control of Egypt in the 1170s. In the eyes of many contemporaries, massacres, such as what happened at Acre, seemed to be part of medieval warfare.

Over time, legends developed about Richard's actions on crusade and his great struggle against Saladin. These stories and pictures like the one below helped to create Richard's reputation as the great warrior king – a brave and heroic soldier who fought against the odds in the Holy Land. In recent years there has been a great deal of debate about Richard's involvement in the Third Crusade.

▲ This map shows the land recovered as a result of the Third Crusade. The Muslims still held Jerusalem and surrounded the Christian lands.

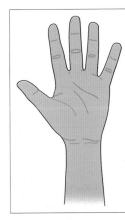

On the one hand …
Some historians have taken a far more critical view of Richard's actions on the crusade. They argue that his achievements in the Holy Land have been exaggerated and that his involvement in the crusade (and subsequent capture on his return home) had negative consequences – causing major financial problems and instability in the Angevin Empire. They also argue that the Third Crusade ended in stalemate – with Jerusalem still in Saladin's hands. They point out that Richard's major success – victory at Acre – was achieved with Philip's help.

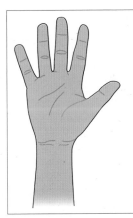

On the other hand …
Other historians have argued that Richard's leadership was often inspired and, given the problems Richard faced, it is amazing that he achieved as much as he did. Richard was able to stop Saladin's advance in the Holy Land. His victories at Arsuf and Jaffa inspired many Christians and raised morale – they also sent a clear message to Saladin that he would face strong resistance if he tried to take the rest of the Holy Land. The eventual truce allowed pilgrims to visit Jerusalem and meant that the Christians had gained control of key ports on the coast.

◀ An illustration from the fourteenth century showing Richard and Saladin in combat. This scene never happened. Richard and Saladin never actually met each other face to face.

5 Richard, John and the loss of Normandy

Events in Normandy dominated the final years of Richard's reign. After a long struggle Richard was able to win back most of the land that Philip had taken while he had been a prisoner in Germany. However, by 1204 John had lost control of Normandy, Philip now dominated the **duchy** and the power of the Angevin Empire had been seriously reduced.

You begin this chapter by exploring the key question:

Why did Richard succeed in Normandy but John fail?

You will start by looking at why Richard, John and Philip II were prepared to fight so hard to control Normandy, before going onto analyse:

- the reasons why Richard was able to win back control of Normandy between 1194 and 1199
- the reasons why John had lost control of Normandy by 1204
- the consequences of the loss of Normandy.

5.1 Competing for Normandy

Why was Normandy so important to Richard, John and Philip?

Economic reasons

- Normandy was a very wealthy area – the revenues it brought the Angevin crown were close to the total raised from the whole of England.
- Normandy had contributed a great deal of money to help pay Richard's ransom.
- Strong trade links existed between Normandy and England.

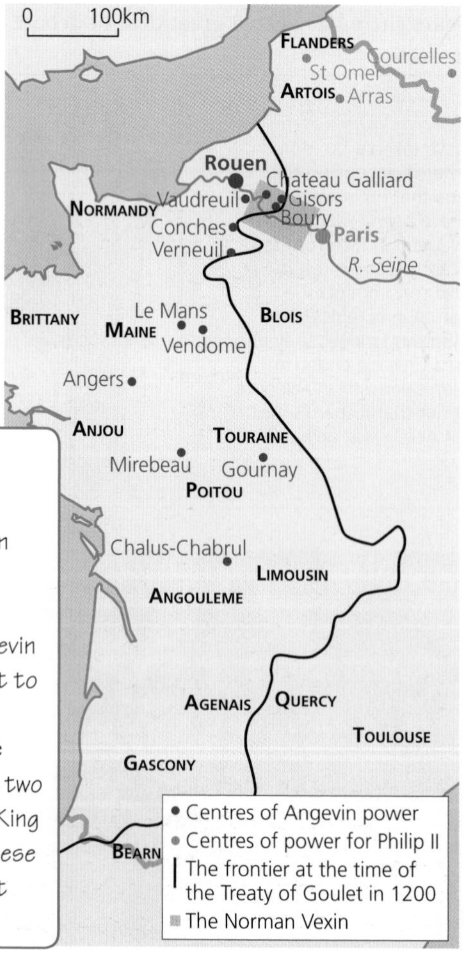

Political reasons

- Many leading English barons controlled lands in Normandy as well as England.
- The loss of Normandy could damage the leading English barons' confidence in their King's ability to protect his people and provide stability.

Strategic reasons

- If the French King gained control of Normandy he could use it as a base from which to launch an invasion of England.
- Normandy was just one day's ride from Paris, the French capital. Philip saw Angevin control of Normandy as a serious threat to his kingdom.
- The key region was an area known as the Norman Vexin. This area lay between the two centres of power – Paris for the French King and Rouen for the Duke of Normandy. These two cities were less than 80 miles apart and connected by the River Seine.

THE IMPORTANCE OF NORMANDY ?

1 What do you think was Philip's main motive for spending such large sums of money fighting for control of Normandy?

2 What do you think was Richard's main motive?

3 Look at the position in 1194 and the biography of Philip II (page 65). Why was Richard in a difficult position? Explain why Phillip was a dangerous opponent and why the position in 1194 did not favour Richard.

Map key:
- Centres of Angevin power
- Centres of power for Philip II
- The frontier at the time of the Treaty of Goulet in 1200
- The Norman Vexin

Map labels: FLANDERS, Courcelles, St Omer, ARTOIS, Arras, Rouen, Chateau Galliard, Vaudreuil, Gisors, NORMANDY, Boury, Conches, Paris, Verneuil, R. Seine, BRITTANY, Le Mans, MAINE, BLOIS, Vendome, Angers, ANJOU, TOURAINE, Mirebeau, Gournay, POITOU, Chalus-Chabrul, LIMOUSIN, ANGOULEME, AGENAIS, QUERCY, TOULOUSE, GASCONY, BEARN

0 100km

Why was Philip II a dangerous opponent?

Read the description below to learn more about Philip II and understand why he was such a problem for Richard.

PHILIP II

BACKGROUND
- Born 1165.
- King of France since 1180.
- Had successfully reduced the power of his own nobles and improved the French system of government

WEALTH IN 1194
- Philip was now wealthier than he had been during the reign of Henry II.
- In 1192 he had taken control of Artois from Flanders. Control of this wealthy area gave Philip the money to wage war even more effectively.

EXPERIENCE BY 1194
- A clever diplomat – Philip had caused problems for Henry II by encouraging Henry's sons to rebel against their father.
- In 1189, Philip joined with Richard to launch a successful attack on Henry II – forcing Henry to retreat and acknowledge Richard as his heir.
- A skilled military leader – particularly at siege warfare. Philip's engineers had played an important role during the capture of Acre during the Third Crusade (see page 52).
- On returning from crusade, Philip had spread a number of rumours against Richard – stories were invented that Richard had been in secret talks with Saladin and plotted to murder Conrad of Montferrat (Philip's choice as the new King of Jerusalem).

ALLIES IN 1194
- Philip had a number of powerful and wealthy allies, including the Count of Toulouse, the Count of Flanders and the Count of Boulogne.

THE POSITION IN 1194

- Philip had made serious inroads into Normandy. He controlled most of Normandy to the east of the River Seine and he had captured important strongholds such as Gisors.
- Philip's army lay within striking distance of Rouen, the capital city.
- Some of the most powerful Norman lords had gone over to Philip's side, hoping to keep control of their lands if, as seemed likely, he eventually took complete control of Normandy.
- In Aquitaine, leading barons were in revolt against Richard.
- Philip had a number of powerful allies (see above). The odds were firmly stacked against Richard.

WINNING BACK NORMANDY

1 Use the timeline on pages 66–67 to identify and make a list of the key turning points in Richard's successful attempt to win back control of Normandy.

2 Look at the list of events that you have decided were the important turning points. Next to each turning point in your list write down the factors causing it. Use the following coding system:
   - ☐ RM = Richard's military skill
   - ☐ RD = Richard's diplomatic skill
   - ☐ RL = Richard's good luck
   - ☐ PE = Philip's errors (poor decisions and mistakes)

   Note: You may decide that more than one factor played a role. If this is the case, put a star next to the factor that you think influenced the event the most.

3 Time to reach an overall decision: Which of the four factors from activity 2 do you think was the most important reason why Richard was successful? Write a paragraph to support your answer.

Visible learning

What is the difference between a turning point and a catalyst?

Some events are so important that they can be called 'turning points' in history. Other events act as catalysts – they speed up changes that are already taking place. A turning point is more important because it changes the way things are going.

5.2 Why was Richard able to win back control of Normandy between 1194 and 1199?

Philip laid siege to Richard's castle of Verneuil. His siege machines succeeded in bringing down the castle wall. Richard arrived at Verneuil just in time, immediately sending a force of knights and crossbowmen to break the French lines and reinforce the garrison defending the castle. Richard sent the rest of his troops to attack Philip's supply lines. These actions forced Philip's army to withdraw. To make matters worse for Philip, he received the news that John was now fighting on his brother's side, and had taken control of Evreux.

John was laying siege to Vandreuil (a key fortress on the border between Normandy and France). Philip attacked John's camp, taking him by surprise and winning a convincing victory. Most of John's infantry and siege artillery were captured. A truce was made between Richard and Phillip which would last until November 1195. Both sides kept the land they held on the day of the truce.

Richard made an alliance with Raymond VI, the new Count of Toulouse. This turned a former enemy into a friend and ally.

| May 1194 | July 1194 | Late July 1194 | 1196 | October 1196 |

Philip advanced west towards the town of Vendome, threatening the whole of the Loire valley. Richard also moved towards Vendome so the two armies, about even in number, were now only a few miles apart. Philip tried to intimidate Richard, sending a messenger to his camp warning him that the French were about to attack. Richard responded with confidence, saying that he was happy to stay and wait for the French attack and that he would call on them in the morning should they not appear! This unsettled Philip. When Richard advanced the following day, the French retreated. Richard set off in pursuit and Philip narrowly evaded capture by hiding in a small church as Richard rode by. Richard did catch Philip's wagon train – seizing horses, tents, siege engines and much of Philip's treasure. This was a humiliating defeat for Philip and he hastily retreated north.

Richard decided to build a stronghold in Normandy to protect Rouen and act as a secure base from which to attack Philip and reconquer the land that had been taken in Normandy. On the right bank of the Seine he built a new town (Petit Andely). On the 300-ft rock overlooking Petit Andely and the River Seine he built the castle of Cháteaux-Gaillard (see below). Richard played a key role in designing the castle, making sure that the defending garrison could cover all approaches. The fortress was built in just two years at a cost of approximately £12,000 (to put this into perspective, in the whole of his reign, Richard spent £7,000 on all of his castles in England).

The importance of Château Gaillard

- The castle defended the route to Rouen.
- It gave Richard a secure base from which to recover the Norman Vexin between 1196 and 1199.
- Men and supplies could be sent here from Rouen, the Norman capital.
- Men and supplies could also arrive at the castle by river. Richard built a fleet of 70 ships which could be based near the castle and, from here, sail directly to England. This meant that the castle provided a link between the Norman frontier and England.

▼ Château Gaillard and the surrounding area.

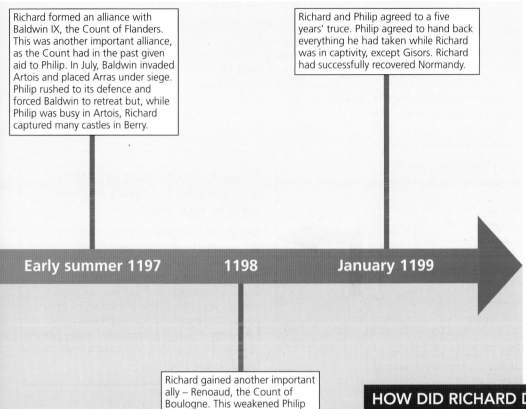

Richard formed an alliance with Baldwin IX, the Count of Flanders. This was another important alliance, as the Count had in the past given aid to Philip. In July, Baldwin invaded Artois and placed Arras under siege. Philip rushed to its defence and forced Baldwin to retreat but, while Philip was busy in Artois, Richard captured many castles in Berry.

Richard and Philip agreed to a five years' truce. Philip agreed to hand back everything he had taken while Richard was in captivity, except Gisors. Richard had successfully recovered Normandy.

Early summer 1197   **1198**   **January 1199**

Richard gained another important ally – Renoaud, the Count of Boulogne. This weakened Philip and, in September, Richard's two new allies (Baldwin and Renoaud) moved into Artois and took control of St Omer. In Normandy, Richard captured Courcelles and Boury. Philip was forced back to his castle at Gisors. Richard continued to gain ground, forcing Philip to agree to peace terms.

HOW DID RICHARD DIE?

In March 1199, Richard went to Aquitaine, where the Count of Angouleme and the Viscount of Limoges had rebelled against him. Richard brought up troops to lay siege to the Viscount's castle at Chalus-Chabrul (see map on page 64). For three days Richard attacked the castle. His crossbowmen forced the defenders to keep their heads down while his sappers undermined the walls.

The castle was on the verge of surrender when, on the evening of 26 March, Richard left his tent to see how the siege was progressing. Daylight was beginning to fade and, because he was not riding into battle, he wore no armour expect for an iron headpiece – relying on his large shield to protect him. Richard had heard that one brave enemy crossbowman, using a frying pan as a shield, had appeared on the ramparts of the castle. As Richard moved towards the castle, this crossbowman aimed an arrow in Richard's direction. Richard, taken by surprise, did not have time to duck behind his shield. The arrow struck his left shoulder. Richard made no sound, not wishing to alarm his men, and calmly returned to his tent. He tried to pull out the bolt but snapped off the wooden shaft, leaving the iron barb deeply embedded in the flesh. A surgeon did manage to remove the bolt and Richard was bandaged up but the wound turned gangrenous and infection spread. Richard died on the evening of 6 April, by which time the castle had fallen to his men.

5.3 Visible learning: Developing independence

The author and editor think that this is the most important page in the book. Why? **?**

At some time in the future you will need the skills to study for yourself, with much less or maybe no help from a teacher. This might be at A level, or if you go to university. The enquiry process you will use in the rest of this chapter will help you work independently and more effectively. Here's the process – in six stages:

THINK BACK AND CONNECT

You can use your findings from your enquiry into why Richard was successful in Normandy to help you develop a hypothesis about why John failed. Look at the factors in the activity on page 65 that explain Richard's success. Were these things missing for John between 1199 and 1204?

Stage 1: Ask questions and choosing an Enquiry Question

Questions focus your work effectively. You know the 'big' question you are investigating – Why did Richard succeed in Normandy but John fail? You have already studied the reasons behind Richard's success. It is now time to explore this key Enquiry Question in the thought bubble.

Why had John lost control of Normandy by 1204?

Did John lack Richard's military skills?
Was John poor at diplomacy and building strong alliances?
Did John suffer from bad luck?
Did Philip become a more powerful and effective opponent?

Stage 2: Suggest a hypothesis in answer to the Enquiry Question

Construct a hypothesis that helps you stay on track as you work.

Stage 3: Research the topic and collect evidence that helps answer the question

Pages 69–74 explore what happened – how John struggled to control his lands on the **Continent** and eventually lost Normandy. It is important to organise your research as you go. Design your own Knowledge Organiser for this enquiry. Check it with your teacher before you start your research.

Stage 4: Revise your hypothesis and get your summary answer clear in your mind

When you complete your research you will need to think again about your hypothesis. How accurate was it? Think carefully about your answer to the Enquiry Question and get your argument clear in your mind. Use the activities on page 75 to help you. Talking it through and debating with others really helps you construct a clear, direct answer to the Enquiry Question.

Stage 5: Communicate your answer

The way you organise and communicate your ideas is very important.

Stage 6: Create material you can revise from effectively

Successful students do not leave revision until the last few weeks before the exam – they revise as they go through the course. They also know how to revise effectively. Some strategies that will help you remember the key points from this chapter are provided on page 77.

5.4 Why had John lost control of Normandy by 1204?

Some historians have argued that John faced a major challenge in keeping the Angevin Empire together and that he deserves a great deal of sympathy for the loss of Normandy in 1204. It is important to start by forming a clear picture of John's position in 1199. How far does this evidence suggest that John was in an unfortunate position?

HOW DIFFICULT WAS JOHN'S POSITION IN 1199?

1 Look at the information cards below and imagine that you are placing them on a set of scales. Which way would the scales tip? In John's favour or Philip's?

2 How far does this information support or challenge your hypothesis from page 68? Does it suggest that John was unlucky and inherited a difficult situation or does it indicate that he was in a strong position in 1199?

When Richard died, the leading barons in Normandy and England quickly showed their support for John. In Aquitaine, Eleanor guaranteed the duchy would go to John.

The taxes introduced by Richard to pay for his overseas wars had been unpopular. By the end of 1198 there was some discontent in England at the weight of the King's financial demands. Richard had taxed more heavily than his father.

There were a substantial number of barons who held land in England and Normandy. These barons had every reason to try and keep England and Normandy together.

Richard's alliances were still intact, so John could call on the Count of Flanders and the Count of Boulogne as his allies.

After Richard's death, the leading men in Brittany chose Arthur (the son of John's deceased elder brother, Geoffrey) as their new ruler, as did many powerful barons in Anjou, Maine and Touraine.

John had a promise of support from Otto IV, the man most likely to become the new German emperor.

Some Normans did not trust John – they remembered how he had plotted against Richard, sided with Philip and not defended the duchy in 1193.

Normandy was well defended – including the impressive new fortress of Château Gaillard.

Philip was an experienced military leader and cunning diplomat.

Philip's wealth had grown and, by 1199, he could match John's financial power (some historians argue Philip was better off).

The loss of Normandy: Stage 1: 1199–1200

John marries Isabella of Angouleme

As soon as he heard of Richard's death, Philip invaded Normandy. Meanwhile, Arthur swore homage to the French King. Arthur posed a significant threat to John. In the minds of some people, he had a better claim than John to be Richard's successor. Arthur was the son of John's older brother.

John acted with impressive speed and was quick to get his authority recognised in Normandy and England. On 27 May he was crowned king at Westminster and, by the end of June, he was back in Rouen with a large army. In the late summer of 1199, John's forces caught up with Philip and pushed him back to Le Mans. Philip decided on a tactical retreat. John seemed to be gaining the upper hand. John's position was strengthened when Arthur's key supporter in Anjou (William des Roches) decided to change sides.

In May 1200 John made peace with Philip through the Treaty of Le Goulet.

THE TREATY OF LE GOULET

- Philip recognised John as Richard's heir.
- Philip recognised John's right to all his Continental possessions. It was agreed that Arthur could hold the Duchy of Brittany, but John would be his overlord. The next day John received Arthur's homage for Brittany.
- The treaty laid down a clear boundary between Normandy and France. Philip gained some land in the Norman Vexin but John remained in control of the key stronghold of Château Gaillard.
- John agreed to pay the massive sum of 20,000 marks for his Continental territories – a payment of relief (see page 35) to Philip as his overlord. Neither Henry nor Richard had done this.
- John agreed that the Counts of Flanders and Boulogne should do homage to Philip. John had ended the alliance system Richard had worked so hard to create.
- The settlement with Philip brought two years of peace – during which John strengthened his control over his Continental possessions.

In 1200, John ended his marriage to Isabella of Gloucester. He married another Isabella, heiress to the county of Angouleme (see map on page 64). The city of Angouleme was crucial for John's control of Poitou and his territories south of Normandy. Bringing the Count of Angouleme on his side by marrying his daughter made good strategic sense. The only problem was that Isabella had been promised in marriage to Hugh de Lusignan – the greatest of all the Poitevin nobles and Count of La Marche. Hugh was an important ally. He may have remained an ally if John had compensated Hugh for the loss of a wife that would have brought him greater wealth and power. However, John failed to offer any form of compensation and his actions forced the Lusignan family into the French camp. They appealed to Philip for help.

LOSING NORMANDY – THE BEGINNING ?

Look at the key events that occurred at the start of John's reign.

1 Did the Treaty of Le Goulet strengthen or weaken John's position?

2 Did John's marriage strengthen or weaken his position?

The loss of Normandy: Stage 2: 1200–02

Philip attacks Normandy

Philip was looking for an opportunity to break John's hold on Normandy. Hugh of Lusignan's appeal to Philip for help gave him that opportunity. Philip ordered John to appear at the French Court to answer the charges against him. When John refused to appear, Philip had the excuse he was looking for to attack John's lands in France. For failing to appear at the French Court, John was sentenced to forfeit all his Continental possessions. In 1202, Philip attacked John's lands in Normandy and, in July of that year, Philip captured Gournay. He cleverly burst the walls of a large dam that lay up-river, causing a flood that destroyed its defensive walls.

John loses allies

In July 1202, Philip followed up the capture of Gournay by taking Arthur's homage for all of John's land in France, apart from Normandy – which Philip was determined to have for himself. He gave Arthur 200 knights and a large sum of money to attack the counties of Anjou and Poitou.

To make matters worse for John, it was at this point that he lost crucial allies. John's greatest supporter in the region, his new father-in-law, the Count of Audemar, died. This left John to face Arthur and the Lusignans in the area south of Normandy without the support of his main ally. John's potential ally to the north of Normandy, the Count of Flanders, left to join the Fourth Crusade. Meanwhile, the Counts of Toulouse and Boulogne (Richard's old allies) switched to Philip's side.

John's daring rescue

Eleanor of Aquitaine, John's mother, saw that her son was in a difficult situation. She travelled to the castle of Mirebeau, intending to help direct operations in Poitiers and defeat Arthur. However, she suddenly found herself besieged by Arthur's army. It seemed only a matter of time before the town fell and she became her grandson's hostage. John quickly gathered his soldiers and dashed to his mother's rescue. The speed of his attack (covering over 80 miles in 48 hours) caught Arthur and his army completely by surprise. John defeated Arthur and Hugh de Lusignan, taking them and many other nobles prisoner.

William des Roches, John's seneschal of Anjou, played a key role in the victory at Mirebeau by leading the attack on Arthur's army. One account states he had three horses killed underneath him, yet continued to fight and lead his troops. However, John took the credit for himself and refused to give William a say in how the prisoners should be treated. William des Roches moved over to the French King's camp. In October, William marched into Angers and took control of the capital.

Despite the loss of Angers, John's prospects still looked good. He still controlled most of Poitou and the two biggest threats to his lands south of Normandy, Hugh and Arthur, had been captured.

PHILIP'S GAINS

1 Look at the events that occurred between 1200 and 1202. Can you find evidence of the following:
  □ Philip being a strong and skilful opponent
  □ John's military mistakes
  □ John's poor diplomacy
  □ John suffering from bad luck?

2 How far does this evidence support or challenge your hypothesis from page 68?

The loss of Normandy: Stage 3: 1203–04

THE LOSS OF NORMANDY

1 Look at the events between 1203 and 1204 (pages 72–74). Can you find evidence of the following:
  - ☐ Philip being a strong and skilful opponent
  - ☐ John's military mistakes
  - ☐ John's poor diplomacy
  - ☐ John suffering from bad luck.

2 How far does this evidence support or challenge your hypothesis from page 68?

Arthur disappears

In 1203 rumours started to spread about what had happened to Arthur since his capture at Mirebeau. Three different contemporary chronicles give different versions of events.

> Ralph of Coggeshall states that John attempted to blind and castrate Arthur.

> The Annals of Margam claim that John, drunk one night after dinner, killed his nephew with his own hands and threw his body, attached to a heavy stone, into the River Seine.

> William the Breton stated that John had taken Arthur out in a boat and then killed him with a sword before dumping the corpse overboard.

Historians cannot always be certain about what happened in the past. Arthur's disappearance is one of history's great mysteries. Arthur was not seen again and people at the time thought that John had murdered his young nephew. Whatever the real story, the consequences of Arthur's disappearance were highly significant. John's cruel treatment of Arthur and other prisoners lost him the support and trust of his barons in France:

- Barons in Brittany believed that John was responsible for Arthur's death and joined Philip.
- The great majority of the Poitevin nobility had friends or relatives taken prisoner by John at Mirebeau. They were shocked and angered when John had even the highest-ranking nobles kept in chains like common criminals.
- John's actions after Mirebeau led to a large number of Norman barons deserting him and joining Philip. These men may have decided it was better to join Philip on the winning side than wait to be beaten fighting for John. Arthur had turned out to be more of a threat to John dead than he had been alive!

1203: Success for Philip

In 1203, Philip conquered Anjou and Maine before turning north towards Normandy. During the summer of 1203, Philip captured Conches, Les Andelys and Vaudreuil. John must have been disappointed to lose Vaudreuil as it was an important and well-stocked stronghold, and even Philip must have expected a lengthy siege of the castle. However, to everyone's surprise, its English commanders (Robert FitzWalter and Saer de Quicy) handed over the castle without putting up a fight.

Philip attacks Château Gaillard

Philip seemed set to conquer Normandy but standing in his way was Château Gaillard, the most technologically advanced fortress in Europe. Set high on a rock above a bend in the River Seine, it seemed to be invincible. At the foot of the rock was a fortified town, Little Andely, and opposite the town was a long narrow island (the Isle of Andely) where Richard had created a crossing protected by a fort.

Philip led his army up the left bank of the Seine – intending to capture the fort on the island first. However, the garrison defending the fort heard news of Philip's attack and destroyed the bridge linking the island to the left bank. Philip had planned for this – he had brought materials to build a new crossing further up the river. He was able to build a **pontoon bridge** and lead the majority of his men across to the eastern bank of the Seine.

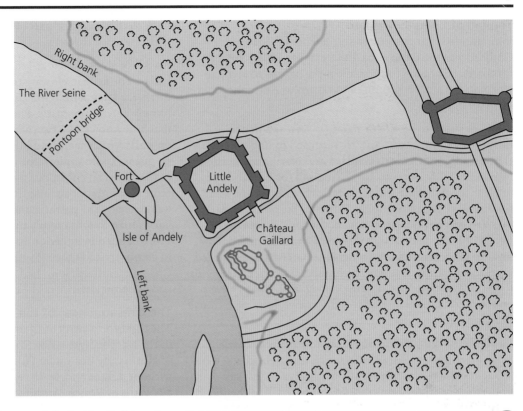

The garrison in the island fort was now surrounded. When news reached John, he planned a daring rescue. Two separate forces would attack the French at night. The first (led by William Marshal) would make its way along the left bank and tackle the French soldiers on that side of the river. The second would attack via the river – using a fleet of ships they would smash the French pontoon and bring supplies to the garrison on the island.

William Marshal's force caught the French as they were sleeping, killing as many as 200 soldiers. The rest of the French force tried to escape across the pontoon bridge but it broke under the strain. The time was right for John's fleet to join the attack and complete the destruction of the pontoon. However, the fleet was nowhere to be seen because the oarsmen were battling against the strong tide. This gave the French on the opposite side of the river time to react. They quickly repaired the pontoon and marched across to attack and defeat Marshal's troops.

By the time John's fleet arrived, the pontoon bridge and both banks of the river were lined with French soldiers. The ships sailed into a storm of arrows and stones. Two ships were sunk, two were captured and the rest retreated. The French set fire to the fort, forcing the garrison defending it to surrender. The French were in total control of the area surrounding Château Gaillard.

DECISION TIME

By the end of 1203 John was in a difficult position. He had a crucial decision to make. Look at his options below. What would you have done next?

- March to Château Gaillard as quickly as possible and confront Philip in a major battle.
- Send a message to Roger de Lacy (the commander of Château Gaillard) instructing him to surrender to Philip.
- Hope that Roger de Lacy's forces could hold out for a long time without your help – giving you time to strengthen your defences in the west of Normandy.
- Return to England and try and persuade more English barons to join your army.
- Return to England and raise taxes to buy foreign mercenaries (professional soldiers) who could strengthen your army.
- Try and lure Philip away from Château Gaillard by attacking his allies in Brittany.

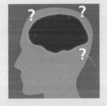

The fall of Château Gaillard

John decided that rushing to the defence of Château Gaillard was too dangerous. In December 1203 John left for England, hoping to persuade more barons to come to Normandy's aid. He promised to return to Normandy, but he never did.

John's decision to leave Normandy is seen as a major mistake by many historians. He returned to England when the defenders of Château Gaillard and Normandy needed him most. John's motives for setting sail for England are unclear. He may have felt personally threatened as he had few friends left in Normandy. However, his position, early in 1204, was not hopeless. Rouen, the capital, was in the hands of Peter de Preaux, a skilled military commander loyal to John. A number of other Norman castles remained loyal too. Château Gaillard, commanded by the courageous Roger de Lacy, was still holding out against Philip. John's presence could have made a real difference, keeping barons in Normandy loyal to his cause.

By February 1204, Philip was ready to storm the castle. Siege machines (ballistae, mangonels and trebuchets) were brought close to the castle walls while French soldiers undertook the dangerous task of trying to fill in the moat protecting the castle. Philip's engineers were able to mine under the foundations of one tower and eventually it collapsed, leaving a hole through which the French could storm. The garrison defending the castle quickly withdrew to the castle's middle bailey. Eventually they were pushed back to the strongest part of the castle – the inner bailey – which housed the keep.

An 8 foot thick, 500 foot-long wall enclosed the inner bailey. The keep itself was surrounded by a 50 foot-wide ditch. De Lacy, with fewer than 180 men, continued to bravely defend the castle. Philip sent forward a siege machine known as a cat (scrofa). This was a reinforced roof on walls which acted as a huge mobile shield – under which engineers could undermine the walls of the defending castle. Then an enormous petraria was used to hurl large stone blocks against the walls. Eventually the wall, weakened by the petraria and Philip's miners, collapsed. De Lacy's men fought on in hand-to-hand combat before being overwhelmed by superior numbers. They were led away in chains. It had taken Philip's army six months to take Château Gaillard. John had failed to take advantage of De Lacy's heroic defence of the castle.

The consequences of the fall of Château Gaillard

The fight for control of Château Gaillard was the key event in the war for Normandy. Within three months the whole of Normandy was under Philip's control. Caen surrendered without a fight and, by the end of May, Philip reached the city walls of Rouen. An agreement was made between Peter de Preaux and Philip that if John did not send aid within 30 days, the city would surrender. Peter knew that only a direct intervention from England could save the situation. Help from John did not come and at the end of June, Rouen surrendered. Normandy was lost, Philip had triumphed.

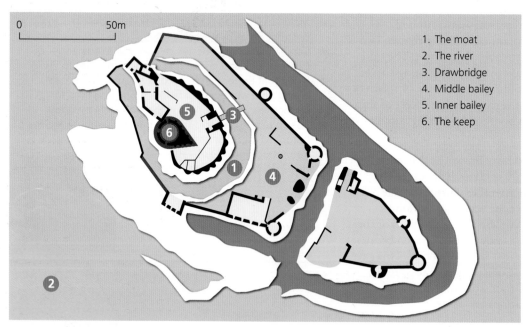

0   50m

1. The moat
2. The river
3. Drawbridge
4. Middle bailey
5. Inner bailey
6. The keep

▲ A plan of Château Gaillard.

5.5 Communicating your answer

Revising your hypothesis and constructing a clear argument

Now you have completed your research you will need to think again about your hypothesis in answer to the question:

Why had John lost control of Normandy by 1204?

Think carefully about your answer to the enquiry question. Revise your hypothesis from page 68 and get your summary answer clear in your mind before you write. This is a really vital stage because one of the biggest mistakes that students make is starting to write without being clear on their line of argument. The activities will help you do that and they will work better if you do them with a partner or in a small group. Talking it through and debating with others really helps you construct a clear and direct answer to the enquiry question.

1 Look at the blue key event cards on the right. Sort them into chronological order and write them down in the first column of the Knowledge Organiser below.

Knowledge Organiser			
Key event	Significance rating and explanation	Factors that influenced the event	Importance rating and explanation

2 In the second column of the Knowledge Organiser, give each event a significance rating. How important was it in deciding why Philip was able to seize control of Normandy? Give it a star rating and explain your decision:
 ■ *** the most significant event
 ■ ** a very significant event
 ■ * quite a significant event

3 Look at the factor diamonds to the right. Which factors do you think influenced each event? Record these factors in the third column of the Knowledge Organiser.

4 For each event, decide how important a factor was. Give it a 'star' rating and explain your decision:
 ■ *** the factor was crucial
 ■ ** the factor was important
 ■ * the factor was quite important

5 Now you should feel fully prepared to answer our enquiry question. If you need more help use the Writing Guide on pages 116–117.

Philip's skill

John's military mistakes

John's poor diplomacy (the loss of key allies)

John's bad luck

Visible learning

Why is it important to prioritise events and causes before you start to write your answer?

1 It is a lot easier to write a good answer that is focused on the question if you have a clear line of argument in your head **before** you begin to write. The activities above help you decide which factors were the most important before you begin your answer. Successful students spend time thinking about their approach to the question before they start to write.

2 Prioritising helps you to select what to include in an exam answer. You will not have time to cover all the key events in the exam. You need to be writing about the really significant events that led to John's loss of Normandy.

Philip captures Gournay

John returns to England

Philip captures Vaudreuil

William des Roches swaps sides and joins Philip

John marries Isabella of Angouleme

Arthur disappears

The Counts of Toulouse and Boulogne become Philip's allies

Philip captures Rouen

Arthur attacks John's lands in Anjou and Poitou

The Count of Audemar dies and the Count of Flanders joins the Fourth Crusade

Philip captures Château Gaillard

5.6 Consequences of the loss of Normandy

The loss of Normandy was a crucial turning point in John's reign for a number of reasons.

- **Collapse of the Angevin Empire**: Philip did not stop at the conquest of Normandy. While John continued to remain in England, Philip's forces took control of much of Poitou. By the end of 1204, only Gascony, the port of La Rochelle and a few strongholds remained in John's hands.
- **Financial problems**: The loss of Normandy meant a significant decrease in the amount of money coming into the royal treasury. Revenues from Normandy had nearly equalled those from England.
- **It shaped how John governed England**: John's main aim was now to recover the lands he had lost. It set him on the road to harsher taxation (see Chapter 6). John raised taxes to build and equip a large army to win back the land Philip had taken.
- **Discontented barons**: A large number of barons had lost lands in Normandy.
- **Threat of invasion**: It was England, not France, which now faced the threat of invasion. Philip's capital, Paris, within just a day's ride of English forces during the reign of Richard, was now safe.
- **Damaged reputation**: John lost the respect of his people. Remember, the main role of a medieval monarch was to protect his lands and be a successful military leader.

Impact on Richard and John's reputations

The loss of Normandy damaged John's reputation at the time. He was criticised by contemporaries and he began to lose the confidence of his barons. In contrast, Richard's successes in Normandy added to the respect that many people at the time had for his military skills and leadership.

Richard's actions in Normandy have also impressed modern historians. Richard is praised for his tactics and diplomatic skills, as well as his bravery and courage. Some have argued that his successes against Philip were a greater achievement than his victories on the Third Crusade.

> Do you agree? How do Richard's victories between 1194 and 1199 compare to his victories at Acre, Arsuf and Jaffa?

John's actions in Normandy divide opinion. Some historians argue that John was unlucky in that leading barons in Normandy turned against him. They also claim that he faced a very difficult opponent because Philip was experienced, well-equipped and determined to destroy the Angevin Empire. However, other historians believe that John could have kept control of Normandy. They are critical of John's military leadership and argue that he showed a lack of courage at crucial times. In particular, they argue that John should have confronted Philip directly in battle during 1203. Instead all he could offer was 'a single, half-hearted attempt to relieve the siege at Château Gaillard' and 'in the end he slunk out of Normandy in December 1203, like a thief in the night'.

RICHARD, JOHN AND NORMANDY

1 John was not there when Château Gaillard and Rouen fell in 1204. Do you think he could have made a difference?

2 Would Richard have reacted differently?

3 Would the eventual outcome have been very different under Richard?

5.6 Visible learning: revise and remember

You may get an exam question like the one below:

'The loss of Normandy was the most important consequence of England's fighting overseas between 1189 and 1204.' How far do you agree? Explain your answer. (16 marks)

You need to be careful with this type of question. Think of it as an 'iceberg' question – there is more to it than meets the eye. In terms of the content focus for the question the bit that you can see is 'the loss of Normandy'. However, you need to spot the part of the question that lurks beneath the water. You need to weigh the importance of the consequence of the loss of Normandy against the importance of other consequences that resulted from England's involvement in wars overseas between 1189 and 1204.

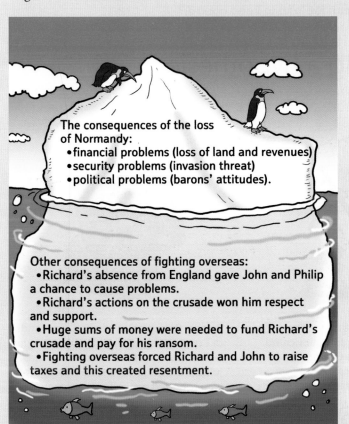

The consequences of the loss of Normandy:
- financial problems (loss of land and revenues)
- security problems (invasion threat)
- political problems (barons' attitudes).

Other consequences of fighting overseas:
- Richard's absence from England gave John and Philip a chance to cause problems.
- Richard's actions on the crusade won him respect and support.
- Huge sums of money were needed to fund Richard's crusade and pay for his ransom.
- Fighting overseas forced Richard and John to raise taxes and this created resentment.

REACHING A JUDGEMENT

Can you think of other consequences of England fighting overseas between 1189 and 1204? If you can, add them to your own copy of the iceberg.

Practice questions

1 Describe two key features of Chateau Gaillard.
2 Explain why people from England joined the Third Crusade.
3 Explain why Richard I joined the Third Crusade.
4 'The main reason for Richard's failure to capture Jerusalem was the strength of Saladin and his army.' How far do you agree? Explain your answer.
5 Explain why Normandy was so important to Richard, John and Philip.
6 Explain why Richard was able to win back Normandy between 1194 and 1199.
7 'John lost Normandy because of his own mistakes.' How far do you agree? Explain your answer.

REVISION CHALLENGE – HOW WELL DO YOU KNOW YOUR KEY BATTLES?

Look at the key battles below. What level of challenge can you complete?

Level 1 – Divide the battles into those fought by Richard and those fought by John.

Level 2 – Place all the battles in chronological order.

Level 3 – Give the dates of as many battles as you can.

Level 4 – What was the outcome of each battle? Who won?

Level 5 – Think about the significance of each battle. Sort the battles into turning points and catalysts. Then decide on the three battles that were the most significant. Others may disagree with you, so prepare for a debate and make sure you can explain your decisions.

Mirebeau	Verneuil	Vaudreuil	Château Gaillard	Jaffa
Messina	Arsuf	Chalus-Chabrul	Gournay	Acre

6 Dispute with the Papacy and worsening relations with the barons

Despite John's loss of Normandy, few people living at the time would have predicted that, in just over ten years' time, John would have lost control of most of England as well. By the summer of 1216 John had quarrelled with the Pope and many of his barons had rebelled against him. John's situation was so desperate that even some of his own household knights had deserted him. The rebel barons had invited Prince Louis of France (Philip II's son) to become king and he now controlled more than half the country. This chapter looks at what caused John's downfall. What made it so difficult for John to keep control?

6.1 John's downfall – forming a hypothesis

FORMING A HYPOTHESIS ?

1 Look back at the main responsibilities of a medieval monarch on page 31. Ultimately, John lost control because he failed to fulfil these responsibilities but **which actions damaged John the most?**

2 Look at the picture summary of what happened between 1205 and 1216.

3 Form a hypothesis – give each action a **potential damage rating** out of five and explain the reason for each score. Remember this is only a hypothesis – you will be able to change your ideas and refine your hypothesis as you study the key events in more detail.

▲ John quarrelled with the Pope. This led to him being excommunicated (expelled) from the Church.

▲ John attempted to win back his lands in France but he failed. In 1214 his army was defeated at the Battle of Bouvines. John also struggled to defeat the barons who rebelled against him, especially when Prince Louis joined them.

▲ John raised taxes to finance expeditions to France in 1206 and 1214. He was constantly looking for ways to raise money and many of his financial policies were very unpopular.

▲ John came down very harshly on people who broke the law, imposing large fines and cruelly imprisoning barons who could not pay debts or who fell out of his favour. Many barons felt that John's actions were very harsh and unfair.

▲ John rarely consulted with his leading barons. He tended to rely on favourites, whom he rewarded at the expense of others.

6.2 Investigations into John's downfall

In Chapter 6 you will carry out two investigations:

1 The dispute with the Papacy: What were the causes of the dispute and how far did it damage John's position?
2 Worsening relations with the barons: Which factor did the most damage to John's relationship with his barons?

Both these developments damaged John's reputation at the time. The dispute with the Papacy and John's actions towards both the Church and his barons were heavily criticised by medieval chroniclers. However, it should be remembered that many of these chroniclers were monks or men who were paid to write their accounts by wealthy barons (or members of their families). This has led some modern historians to challenge whether their criticisms of John are justified. They argue that John faced difficult decisions and that disputes with the Pope and the barons were inevitable and not entirely John's fault.

DECISION TIME

Below are two important decisions that John had to make. What would you have decided to do in these circumstances? Explain each choice that you make.

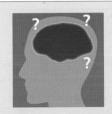

Decision 1: 1205 – Who decides on the new Archbishop of Canterbury?	Decision 2: 1207 – How do you raise money to build an army strong enough to take back your lands in France?
Background	**Background**
• The Archbishop of Canterbury was the most important religious figure in the country. He had responsibility for twelve other bishops. • An archbishop who had a bad working relationship with his king could cause major problems. Henry II's quarrel with Thomas Becket was still fresh in everyone's mind (see page 29). • Hubert Walter, the Archbishop of Canterbury, died. John wanted to replace him with John de Gray (the Bishop of Norwich). • The other person who had a major interest in the appointment of the Archbishop of Canterbury was the Pope. He claimed the right to authorise the appointment of all archbishops. Pope Innocent III wanted to choose his own candidate – Stephen Langton. • Langton had connections with France and had lived in Paris. John was very suspicious of him.	• By 1206, John's lands in Gascony and Poitou were under threat. John successfully defended Gascony and advanced into Poitou. Philip responded by marching south from Paris, forcing John and his smaller army to retreat. • In October 1206 a truce between John and Philip left Philip in control of all his conquests – Anjou, Maine and Normandy. If John wanted to recover these lands he needed a bigger army and allies. This required a large amount of money, so raising cash would be John's priority from 1207. Which of these options would you have taken?
Options	**Options**
1 Give in to the Pope – agree that Langton becomes the next archbishop. 2 Stand up to the Pope – insist that John de Gray becomes archbishop. 3 Let the monks at Canterbury decide who should be the next archbishop. 4 Ask the twelve other bishops to choose the next archbishop.	1 Increase fines (amercements) for anyone who breaks the law. 2 Introduce a general, one-off tax on everyone (the amount people had to pay would depend on the moveables they owed and the money they received in rents). 3 Demand that your sheriffs collect more money from the counties. 4 Demand money from your barons in return for your goodwill and support in court cases. 5 Increase the amount of money that barons have to pay you for wardships and when they inherited land and estates (reliefs) (see page 15). 6 Demand more money from the widows of tenants-in-chief who want to inherit their husband's land without remarrying. 7 Increase tallages (taxes) on towns and cities – especially London.

6.3 The dispute with the Papacy: What were the causes of the dispute and how far did it damage John's position?

After the death of Hubert Walter, John was determined that he alone would decide the next Archbishop of Canterbury. His choice for archbishop was one of his most trusted advisers, John de Gray, Bishop of Norwich. John knew it was important to have a good working relationship with the Archbishop of Canterbury because he would have heard of the trouble caused by Thomas Becket for his father, Henry II (see page 29). In contrast to Becket and Henry II, Hubert Walter had worked well with both Richard and John. He was a skilled administrator and adviser, helping to rule England while they were out of the country.

John wanted to make sure that the new archbishop would be someone whom he could rely on. John believed that it was his right to choose bishops and that the election of bishops was an important source of royal patronage – a way of rewarding those loyal to him and ensuring that those in positions of power would follow his wishes.

John put pressure on the monks at Canterbury to agree to his choice of archbishop. He then wrote to Pope Innocent III informing him of the decision to appoint John de Gray. By June 1207, John was in conflict with the Pope. Innocent III ordered John to make Stephen Langton archbishop. Innocent III and Langton had studied together at the University of Paris and formed a strong friendship. The Pope wrote to leading bishops in England asking them to support Langton. John did not trust Langton and refused to follow the Pope's orders.

THE QUARREL WITH THE POPE

1 Summarise the key reasons for the dispute between John and the Papacy.

2 Study the consequences of the dispute on page 81. How far did it damage John's position? Choose your position on the 'damage thermometer' to the right and then explain your decision.

5 = Devastating consequences – the main reason for John's downfall

4 = Damaging consequences – a very significant reason for John's downfall

3 = Harmful consequences – an important reason for John's downfall

2 = Limited consequences

1 = Inconsequential

The Damage Thermometer

Consequence 1: The Interdict

By 1208 the Pope had lost patience with John's refusal to accept Langton and declared an Interdict on England. The Interdict meant the ending of church services, which made it difficult to baptise infants and bury the dead in churchyards – bodies were laid to rest in woods, ditches and by the roadside without the services of a priest.

However, many aspects of religious life continued unaffected. Not everyone followed the Pope's Interdict. The evidence suggests that many individual churchmen continued to carry out services throughout the period. Most of the clergy and many monks seem to have been on John's side. However, only two bishops – John de Gray and Peter of Winchester – remained in England. The rest moved overseas.

Consequence 2: John seizes Church property

John responded to the Interdict by seizing Church property. Instructions were sent out to his sheriffs and officials in the countryside to confiscate the property of any of the clergy who opposed the King. Some bishoprics were placed in the hands of John's supporters and favourites. The land of those bishops and abbots who sided with the King stayed safe.

A great deal of Church property found its way into the King's hands. John made a lot of profit from it. He thought that he could use Church property as if it were his own. Bishops, like other crown tenants, held their lands in return for service. In John's mind, because these bishops were no longer carrying out church services they had no right to the property. Those bishops who supported the Pope lost their lands. The same went for abbots and monks who refused to carry out services.

Consequence 3: John is excommunicated

In January 1209, the Pope threatened that if John did not appoint Stephen Langton as Archbishop of Canterbury within three months he would be excommunicated. This was dangerous for John. It would place him outside the Church and he would no longer have the Pope's support or protection. Popes who had excommunicated rulers had gone on to declare that the specific king no longer had the right to rule and even encouraged fellow Christians to make war on them. Despite the dangers, John refused to back down and, in November, he was excommunicated.

John does not seem to have been troubled by excommunication – he took the opportunity to continue to seize Church property and lands and made huge profits over the next few years. It is estimated that an extra £65,000 found its way into the royal treasury, helping to boost the funds available for war. In addition, John's excommunication did not result in him losing support from people in England. As you will see, the barons had different reasons for rebelling against their king.

Consequence 4: Reconciliation with the Pope

Eventually John and Pope Innocent III settled their differences. In May 1213, John agreed that Stephen Langton could become Archbishop of Canterbury. He even went so far as to accept Innocent III as his overlord and agree that his kingdoms of England and Ireland would be held from the Pope as a fief. In June, John ordered that all Church lands that had been seized in the name of the king should be returned. In July, Stephen Langton arrived in England and ended John's excommunication.

Why did John back down after spending so long in dispute with the Pope? The main reason is that by 1213 John's circumstances had changed and he felt in a vulnerable position. In 1213, John became aware that Philip II was planning an invasion of England. John needed the Pope's support. By accepting the Pope as his overlord, John placed himself under the protection of the Pope. This was a clever political move as it meant that any attack by the French on John would also be seen as an attack on the Pope and the Roman Catholic Church. John had managed to resolve the dispute with the Papacy before it became a serious threat to his position.

6.4 Worsening relations with the barons: Which factor did the most damage to John's relationship with his barons?

John's relationship with his barons went from bad to worse between 1205 and 1215, ending in rebellion and a bloody civil war. What caused the barons to rebel? In this enquiry you will study and evaluate the damage done by four factors to John's relationship with the barons. These can be remembered as the 4Fs:

Financial impositions – John was constantly looking for ways to raise money so he could build up an army large enough to win back his lands in France. On page 79 we asked you to decide on which options you would have taken to raise money. John used all seven methods (and many more) to increase the money coming into the royal treasury. These methods were seen as financial impositions because they placed a big burden on the barons and the King imposed them; they were not introduced with the agreement of the barons.

Fairness – John seemed to use his power arbitrarily and did not seem to make consistent and fair judgements. He introduced cruel punishments for those who fell out of royal favour. This made many barons feel insecure and threatened.

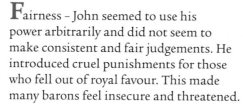

Favourites – John never managed his barons effectively. He rarely consulted them on important decisions and instead he relied on a small group of favourites to advise him.

France – John failed to win back his lands in France, despite spending large sums of money on an enormous army and winning over allies.

What mattered to the barons?

Developing a clear enquiry question is the first step in the enquiry process. The next step is to develop a hypothesis. In order to do this you need to understand what mattered to the barons. What would please them or make them less likely to rebel? What would make them angry?

Things that would please a baron …

– Keeping or increasing your land and wealth.

– Being trusted by the king – this could result in you receiving favours from the king, such as important positions or land.

– Feeling that your family is safe and secure.

– Success in war: an opportunity to gain money or land.

Things that would make a baron angry …

– Losing your wealth and lands.

– Unfair treatment by the king: your advice being ignored, or you being punished.

– Your family being badly treated by the king.

– Failure in war: the threat of invasion.

WHY DID THE BARONS REBEL?

1 Create your hypothesis. Use the sentence starters below to summarise your ideas.

I think that the factor that damaged John's relationship with his barons the most was …

This is because …

2 Use pages 84–90 to research the role played by each factor. Use the Knowledge Organiser below to organise your notes as you carry out your research.

Factor	Evidence that it caused damage	Case study evidence – barons that were affected	Damage rating
Finance			
Favourites			
Fairness			
France			

Pages 86–87 are very important. Here you will be able to study why individual barons rebelled against John. You can use this evidence to provide specific examples to support your arguments.

Use the damage thermometer, right and on page 80, to decide on your rating. Make sure that you think about how you would justify this rating if it is challenged by your teacher or someone else in your class.

3 You have already looked at one of the factors. On page 40 you looked at John's financial policies from 1207 to 1214. Read this page again and use it to start to fill in column 2 for the 'Finance' factor. You will continue to analyse the importance of this factor on the next page.

5

4

3

2

1

The Damage Thermometer

Factor 1: Finance

Key question: How much damage did John's financial policies do to his relationship with the barons?

JOHN'S FINANCIAL POLICIES ?

1 Match each of John's financial policies in Box A to one or more consequences in Box B.
2 Use this information to finish filling in column 2 of your Knowledge Organiser on page 83.

Visible learning

Focusing on consequences

Remember that in this enquiry you are evaluating which factor did the most damage to John's relationship with his barons. It is not enough to simply read the information on page 82 and describe what John did. You need to focus on the consequences of these actions.

> John's actions ⟶ Consequence

One of John's financial policies was to …   *This led to …*

BOX A: JOHN'S FINANCIAL IMPOSITIONS

1 Sheriffs were put under pressure to collect more money from the counties.
2 In 1207, John introduced a new tax called 'The Thirteenth' – everyone had to pay a thirteenth of the value of their rents and moveables to the king.
3 The Thirteenth was introduced without agreement from the leading barons.
4 John took large sums of money in the form of taxation and fines from the towns and cities. He demanded particularly large sums from London and Lincoln.
5 John made sure that the Exchequer worked hard to calculate exactly what individual barons owned. Their debts were added together in one lump sum and the crown seized the barons' lands if they did not repay the debt quickly enough.
6 John restricted what people could do in the royal forests. People were punished heavily if they used forest land to grow crops or for hunting. The heaviest fines were levied in Yorkshire and Northumberland.

BOX B: CONSEQUENCES

a) Barons felt insecure and threatened – many were in debt to the Crown and feared that their land could be taken from them.
b) Anger grew in England's major towns and cities. Both Lincoln and London became rebel bases during the civil war.
c) The barons felt John was becoming a tyrant – ruling on his own without consulting them on key decisions.
d) Resentment and anger grew particularly strong in the North of England. Yorkshire and Northumberland provide the greatest number of rebels in 1215 when the barons finally turned against their king.
e) John's royal officials and judges became very unpopular as they raided homes to try and find possessions that people had hidden in order to pay less tax.
f) Many sheriffs became unpopular as they exploited people in the counties – seizing wood, property and even threatening people with trial if they did not pay extra funds.

Factor 2: Favourites

Key question: How much damage did John's use of favourites to help him rule the country do to his relationship with the barons?

John found it difficult to trust his barons. This meant that he tended to rely almost entirely on those closest to him for advice. John rewarded these royal 'favourites' handsomely. The consequence was that many barons felt excluded from positions of power and influence. They felt that John was using his power arbitrarily – taking decisions that benefited the king and his close associates but nobody else.

There was a lot of jealousy concerning John's **ministers** and **agents**. They were hated because of their ruthless actions and also because of the rewards they gained. The leading barons expected that the king would use his powers of **patronage** to reward a wide circle of people. However, John tended to reward only those closest to him. To make matters worse, some of John's favourites were seen as 'foreigners' – men like Peter des Roches, John's choice as Bishop of Winchester, came from Touraine, while other important officials came from Poitou.

JOHN'S USE OF FAVOURITES AND LACK OF FAIRNESS

John's financial policies created a lot of opposition among the barons, but they were not the only factor behind John's downfall. John's government also collapsed because it had too narrow a support base. John's enemies among the barons far outnumbered his friends. Why was this?

1 How would John's reliance on favourites and the cruelty he displayed to those who fell out of favour make the barons feel? Choose three words from the list below and explain your choice.

angry, bemused, scared, insecure, frightened, furious, jealous, ignored, pleased, unimpressed, unbothered, apathetic

2 Use this information to fill in column 2 of your Knowledge Organiser on page 83 for the 'Favourites' and 'Fairness' factors.

Factor 3: Fairness

Key question: How much damage did John's treatment of William de Briouze and his family do to his relationship with his barons?

William de Briouze had served in Richard I's army and was very close to John at the start of his reign. William was well rewarded for his loyalty and became one of the leading barons in the land. William was Lord of Briouze in Normandy. He also controlled land in Sussex and on the border with Wales. In 1202, John granted William lands in Ireland. John hoped that his presence there would keep the native Irish rulers under control. William promised to pay John 5,000 marks for the grant of this land, which he agreed to pay at 1,000 marks per year. By 1207 William had only paid 700 marks.

In 1208, John tried to force William to pay the debts he owed the Crown by attempting to seize Briouze's chattels (possessions). When Briouze resisted this, all his lands in England and Wales were taken into the King's hands. Briouze fled to Ireland with his wife and eldest son (also called William). When John led an expedition to Ireland in 1210, Briouze left Ireland, spending the remaining years of his life in exile in France. William's wife (Matilda) and son fled to Scotland, only to be captured and brought before the King. It is generally believed that John had Matilda de Briouze and her eldest son starved to death. The following is a contemporary account of what happened:

> He [John] imprisoned Matilda and her son at Corfe Castle and ordered that a sheaf of oats and one piece of raw bacon be given to them. He did not allow them to have any more meat. After eleven days, the mother was found dead between her son's legs. Her son, who was also dead, was found sitting straight, bent against the wall. So desperate was the mother that she had eaten her son's cheeks.

John claimed that his actions were justified by William's non-payment of debts and that the punishment was 'in accordance with the custom of the kingdom and the law of the exchequer'.

John's use of arbitrary power

John's treatment of William de Briouze and his family is a good example of John's use of arbitrary power. John's actions seemed to suggest that he thought that he could act in any manner he wanted without respect for the law or the barons themselves. John's use of arbitrary power made the barons feel very vulnerable. He introduced harsh fines and raised taxes without negotiating with or even consulting the barons. John showed little concern for barons' rights and the nature of punishments seemed to be decided by the King himself. John's treatment of William de Briouze and his family became very well-known and a major talking point in the kingdom. It sent out a clear and chilling message to any baron who owed the King money or fell out of royal favour; if John could treat one of his leading men in this disgraceful way, no baron or anyone in their family appeared to be safe.

Visible learning

Using specific examples to support your arguments

You have now looked at three out of the four factors that damaged John's relationship with his barons. You should feel confident that you can explain how each factor angered the barons. However, good historians support their arguments with specific examples. This makes your argument stronger and helps you win debates against other people who might disagree with your interpretation.

You can use the case studies on pages 86–87 to find out about how individual barons were affected by John's rule. All of these men ended up rebelling against John but what was their main motive? What had John done to turn so many of his leading barons against him?

◀ A drawing by the thirteenth-century chronicler, Matthew Paris, showing people being tortured during the reign of King John.

THE BARONS' MOTIVES

Read the case studies on these two pages. Which factors may have influenced each baron's decision to rebel? Place each baron in a copy of the Venn diagram below. Remember that they may have had more than one reason to rebel, so think carefully about where you place them.

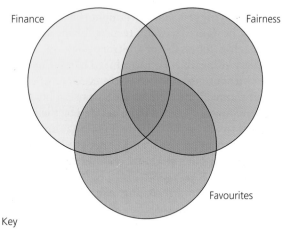

Finance

Fairness

Favourites

Key

Finance – Barons affected by John's financial policies.

Favourites – Barons who may have expected John to favour them but were instead ignored.

Fairness – Barons who felt that John had treated them cruelly or shown them a lack of respect.

▲ We do not know what the individual barons looked like as there are no recorded descriptions or portraits.

Case studies: What turned individual barons against King John?

Eustace de Vesci

- In his forties.
- Lord of Alnwick in Northumberland.
- Married an illegitimate daughter of William the Lion, King of Scotland.
- Used by John to help negotiations with the Scots.
- Rumoured at the time that John had made advances on his wife.
- Owed money to Jewish moneylenders.

Gilbert de Gant

- In his mid-thirties.
- Owned land in south Lincolnshire.
- John had failed to support his claim to the earldom of Lincolnshire.
- Owed £800 to Jewish moneylenders. The debt was taken over by the King and he has given just two years to pay it off.

Richard de Percy

- In his forties.
- Held land in Yorkshire.
- Owed money to the Crown; pressure was put on him to pay back his debts and the rate was set at £400 per year.

Roger de Montbegon

- In his fifties.
- Held land in Lancashire, Yorkshire, Nottinghamshire and Lincolnshire.
- He had supported John's rebellion in 1194 (and was one of the leading defenders of Nottingham castle – see page 62).
- When John became king, Roger may have been hoping to prosper, but this did not happen. In 1204, John seized control of Roger's land as a punishment for failing to come to Court.

John de Lacy

- In his mid-twenties.
- His father had been the defender of Château Gaillard (see page 74) and an important member of John's administration.
- When his father died he was initially too young to inherit so his lands in Lancashire and Yorkshire had been placed in wardship.
- In 1213 he had to agree to a fine of £4,600 to gain his inheritance.
- He gained his lands from the King on very strict terms – John would keep Pontefract and Donington Castles until de Lacy repaid the debt he owed.

Nicholas de Stuteville

- In his mid-fifties.
- Held land in Cumberland and Yorkshire.
- Succeeded to his lands in 1205 – paying the enormous sum of £6,600 to John.
- As a guarantee for repayment he was forced to surrender Knaresborough and Boroughbridge Castles to the King. He never recovered these lands and his debts rose to £10,000.

Robert FitzWalter

- In his mid-thirties.
- Lord of Dunmow in Essex and Baynard's Castle in the city of London.
- John had given him Hertford Castle, but then took it away from him in 1209.
- Robert claimed that John had tried to seduce his daughter.
- It is also claimed by one contemporary chronicler (the Anonymous of Bethune) that John had threatened to hang Robert's son-in-law during a quarrel at court.

Roger de Cressy

- In his mid-thirties.
- His father (Hugh de Cressy) had been close to Henry II. Hugh had loyally supported the King when Henry's sons and some barons rebelled against him in 1173–74.
- Held land in East Anglia.
- In 1207 he was punished with a £800 fine for marrying an heiress without the king's permission.
- The lands of Roger and the heiress were seized until Roger promised to pay £800 to get his lands back.

Geoffrey de Mandeville

- In his mid-twenties.
- Son of John's justiciar (Geoffrey FitzPeter – who died in 1213).
- Geoffrey had taken the surname Mandeville because his father had claimed, through marriage, the Mandeville Earldom of Essex.
- Mandeville's first wife was the daughter of Robert FitzWalter (and it was rumoured that John had tried to seduce her).
- After his wife's death, Geoffrey agreed to pay £13,300 to marry Isabella of Gloucestershire. Geoffrey was told to pay the money in ten months.
- One account states that Mandeville entered the marriage unwillingly, and that John had promised him the title of Earl of Essex as part of the agreement, threatening him with the loss of the whole Mandeville inheritance if he did not agree.
- Geoffrey was never granted the title and, in February 2014, his lands in Gloucestershire were seized.

William de Mowbray

- In his forties.
- Held land in Yorkshire, Lincolnshire and Leicestershire.
- His family had rebelled against Henry II in 1173–74, but his father had accompanied Richard on crusade.
- In 1200, William offered £1,300 to John, hoping that the King would support him in a dispute with William de Stuteville about who had the rights to a barony. John accepted the offer, but his Court declared in favour of Stuteville.
- Mowbray's 'debt' to King John remained on record, but initially he was not asked to pay the £1,300 he had offered John. Mowbray must have been shocked when, in 1208, he was told to pay off the debt at a rate of £100 per year. He had to borrow the money from Jewish moneylenders.

LOOKING CLOSELY AT THE BARONS

1 Can you see any patterns in the case studies of the barons who rebelled against John?
2 Think about the following:
   - Where they lived – did they all tend to come from the North of England?
   - Family history – did they come from families who had a tradition of rebelling against the king?
   - Age – were most of them young men, out to make a name for themselves?
   - They owed money to the king?
   - They had lost land?
3 Fill in column 3 of your Knowledge Organiser from page 83.

The 1212 plot to assassinate John

Before 1212 John faced threats from William the Lion (King of Scotland) and a rebellion in Wales, led by Llywelyn (Prince of Gwynedd). However, John dealt with both threats successfully. In 1209, he marched north with a large army, forcing William the Lion to accept humiliating and costly peace terms. William accepted John as his overlord and handed over two of his daughters as hostages as a guarantee of future good behaviour. In 1211, John launched an attack on Llywelyn's principality in Snowdonia, forcing the Welsh to retreat into the mountains. Llywelyn was forced to seek a peace settlement. He had to surrender hostages (including his son) to John.

In the summer of 1212, John was planning a new campaign to strengthen his control of Wales when, to his complete surprise, he learnt of a plot to assassinate him. Immediately he called the expedition off. The plot was led by Robert FitzWalter and Eustace de Vesci – both ranked among the most powerful men in England.

The barons involved in the plot had planned to murder John in Wales or desert him and let the Welsh do their work for them. They then intended to elect a new king. John acted quickly, dismissing the baronial army and bringing in foreign mercenaries to protect himself. John then marched north. Within ten days, John's forces had taken de Vesci's castle at Alnwick. De Vesci was forced to flee to Scotland while FitzWalter escaped to France. The speed of John's response had stopped an open rebellion.

What were the consequences of the plot?

1 John became fully aware of the threat posed by his barons. He had never really trusted them and the plot seemed to confirm his suspicions. John came to rely more and more on his favourites and foreign mercenaries.
2 In 1213 John made a number of concessions designed to prop up support for his rule. He reformed the administration of the forests and, in the north of England, dismissed some of his unpopular sheriffs.
3 The plot, combined with the threat of invasion from France, also encouraged John to come to an agreement with the Pope in 1213 (see page 81).
4 The plot encouraged Philip II to continue with his plans to invade England and place his eldest son, Louis, on the throne. However, his plans came to nothing. In May, the English navy caught the French fleet by surprise while they were anchored at Damme (the main port for the city of Bruges in Flanders). Most of the French fleet was captured or destroyed, ending the threat of an invasion.

The position in 1214

The plot to assassinate John had been carried out in secret and it is difficult to calculate how many barons were involved. Given John's actions towards his barons, it is perhaps surprising that it took until 1215 for a large number of them to openly rebel.

TIME TO REBEL? **?**

Why might barons be wary of rebelling against John? Look at the reasons below. Rank them in order of importance.

a) John had led successful military campaigns in Scotland (1209), Ireland (1210) and Wales (1211).
b) John had quickly crushed the barons who plotted against him in 1212.
c) The king was God's representative on earth and, by 1213, he had the support of the Pope.
d) Fear of punishment – the barons would have heard the story of what happened to William de Briouze's family.
e) John was very wealthy and could pay for foreign mercenaries.
f) There was no obvious successor to John. Arthur had been murdered and John's son was too young to rule.

Factor 4: France

Key question: How much damage did John's failure to recapture his lands in France do to his relations with his barons?

In the spring of 1214 many barons would have been wary of joining an open rebellion against John, or even trying to persuade him to change the way he ruled the country. Discontent and anger had been building up for a long time but, like a bonfire, it needed a spark to ignite it. The spark came when John's plans to reclaim his lands in France ended in complete failure in the summer of 1214.

Why did John feel confident of success?

In 1214 John had a number of reasons for feeling confident about winning back the territory he had lost at the start of his reign.

Alliances
John had formed alliances with Otto of Brunswick (the Holy Roman Emperor) and the Counts of Boulogne, Flanders and Holland. This meant that he had the support of the leading figures to the north of France.

Support of most of his barons
Despite some opposition to the campaign in England, John was joined on his expedition to France by a large number of his barons, as well as his household knights.

Money and mercenaries
The large sums of money John had raised through his financial policies meant that he could afford to supply a large army and buy in foreign mercenaries.

Tactics
John's plan was to attack Philip on two fronts, forcing him to divide his forces. The Earl of Salisbury was sent with an English force to Flanders, where he joined forces with the Emperor and the Counts of Flanders, Boulogne and Holland. Meanwhile, John landed in the south at La Rochelle.

Why did things go wrong?

At first things went well for John. He captured a number of castles and gained control of much of Poitou. In June he crossed the Loire and reached Angers (the capital of Anjou). However, he was still 80 miles from the border with Normandy and it was at this point that Philip's son, Louis, was sent to halt his advance. Both Louis and John appeared ready for what would have been a decisive battle. Louis led the smaller army and John appears to have been keen to fight. However, John's Poitevin allies were not prepared to risk everything in a battle. Seriously weakened by their refusal to meet Louis in battle, John fled south, leaving behind siege engines, tents, clothes and valuables. Louis quickly took control – retaking castles that had been lost in John's advance. By July, John was back where he had started at La Rochelle. John's campaign was over and everything now depended on his allies in the north.

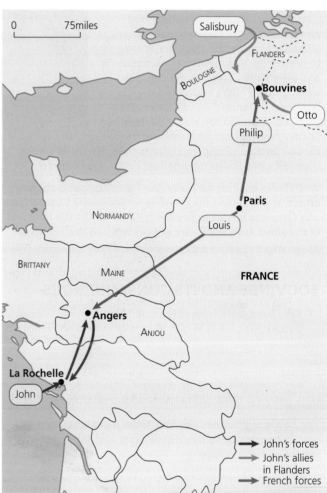

▲ This map shows the movements of the armies of King John and his allies, and of the French armies before the battle of Bouvines in 1214.

THINK BACK AND CONNECT

Look back at the main duties and responsibilities of a medieval king on page 31.

Why would defeat in France damage John's relationship with his barons?

THE BATTLE OF BOUVINES, 1214

John's allies in the north did face a decisive battle. It was perhaps the most significant moment in John's life and he was not there. Instead he was 400 miles away from the battle that would determine his future. It is estimated that John's allies had an army of 1,400 knights and 7,500 infantry. Philip's army totalled around 1,400 knights and 6,000 infantry.

The battle took place on 27 July outside the village of Bouvines (on the border between France and Flanders). The battle was a very close run thing. The allied commanders planned to target Philip on the battlefield. German foot soldiers, armed with pikes and billhooks, managed to drag Philip head first from his horse and were within seconds of killing him when one of Philip's household knights launched a dramatic rescue. As French trumpets sounded the alarm, Pierre Tristan jumped from his horse and put himself between Philip and his attackers. He bravely held them off while Phillip mounted his horse and escaped.

With Phillip back on his horse, the French began a counter attack. In the centre, the Emperor's forces were pushed back and Otto was forced to flee the battlefield. On the left flank of the allied army the Count of Flanders had lost his horse

▲ The image shows King Philip unseated from his horse at the Battle of Bouvines.

and was fighting on foot. Finally, slowed down by serious wounds and exhaustion, he was forced to surrender. On the right flank the Earl of Salisbury and the Count of Boulogne were taken prisoner. Philip was victorious and John's dreams of reclaiming Normandy lay in tatters.

BOUVINES AND ITS CONSEQUENCES

1 Why have some historians argued that John came close to success with his 1214 plan to regain his lands in France?

2 Look at the consequences of John's failure in France in the box below. Use this information to fill in column 2 of your Knowledge Organiser on page 83.

THE IMPACT OF THE FAILURE TO REGAIN NORMANDY

The Battle of Bouvines was one of the most important battles fought during the Middle Ages and its impact was felt throughout Europe.

1 French dominance in western Europe

If his allies had won the battle, John would have been the dominant power in western Europe. Instead, France emerged from the battle as the leading power. Otto lost the German crown to Frederick, who was an ally of Philip. The Count of Flanders was forced to accept a humiliating peace treaty that left Philip in control of much of Flanders.

2 Angry barons in England

A great victory in 1214 would have done a lot to improve John's relationship with his barons. Those who had held land in Normandy at the start of his reign would have been pleased to reclaim their estates. Victory would have also provided some justification for the enormous sums John had raised from his barons to pay for the expedition. However, when John arrived back in England in October his money was gone. Everything he had been working towards for ten years was in ruins. If his allies had won at Bouvines, John's return to England would have been met with great celebration; instead his return was met with outright rebellion.

In the autumn of 1214 it is believed that the rebel barons met at Bury St Edmunds. By this point they were forging links with John's enemies in Wales, France and Scotland. In January 1215 the rebel barons met with John in London. They demanded that John agree to uphold the laws and freedoms written down in Henry I's coronation charter. When John did not respond to their demands the barons moved into open rebellion. You will study what happened next in Chapter 7.

6.5 Visible learning: Evaluating factors

It is now time to evaluate the factors that damaged John's relationship with his barons. You will need to prioritise the factors and reach a damage rating on the thermometer. Before you complete your Knowledge Organiser from page 83 by filling in column 4, look at other people's opinions of the key factors that led to John's barons turning against him.

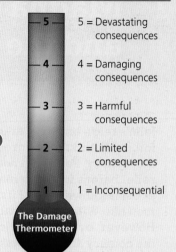

5 = Devastating consequences

4 = Damaging consequences

3 = Harmful consequences

2 = Limited consequences

1 = Inconsequential

The Damage Thermometer

EVALUATING INTERPRETATIONS

1 Read the interpretations below. What factors are put forward in each interpretation as the main reason for John's worsening relationship with the barons?

2 Look at your Knowledge Organiser. Which interpretation do you think is supported by the strongest evidence? Which interpretation do you think is the weakest?

3 Fill in column 4 of your Knowledge Organiser. Make sure you explain your 'damage' rating.

Interpretation A

People were growing increasingly unhappy at the number of foreign mercenaries in the country. They were angered by John's policy of placing them in high office at the expense of English barons. This was the key cause of John's deteriorating relationship with his barons.

Interpretation B

The year 1214 proved to be crucial in John's reign. John earned himself the reputation of a loser. The Battle of Bouvines shattered his authority and meant that he would never be respected by the barons.

Interpretation C

The barons simply did not trust John. This was because of his character and the way he abused royal power. His treatment of William de Briouze was the greatest mistake John made during his reign. It became a major talking point in the kingdom. It made the barons feel very vulnerable. If John could treat one of his leading barons in this disgraceful way, no baron or anyone in their family appeared to be safe.

Interpretation D

Finances lay at the root of John's problems. Scutage fees, fines and taxes hit record highs and the money was collected in a ruthless way by royal officials. John had raised an enormous sum of money and, after his failure in France, he had nothing to show for it.

Interpretation E

John's character itself would not have provoked the barons into rebellion. Nor would his financial demands. It was the two together that destroyed John's relationship with his barons.

Practice questions

In the exam you could be asked an 'explain' or 'judgement' question about John's worsening relations with his barons. Use your Knowledge Organiser and the advice in the guidance pages (112–22) to plan how you would answer the two questions below.

1 Explain why John's relationship with his barons worsened between 1205 and 1215. (12 marks)

2 'King John's financial policies did the most damage to John's relationship with his barons.' How far do you agree? Explain your answer. (16 marks)

THINK BACK AND CONNECT

The second practice question is another example of an 'iceberg question' (see page 77). Remember that to effectively answer this question you need to explore the part of the question that 'lurks beneath the water' – the role of other factors.

You need to weigh the importance of each of these other factors against the impact that John's financial policies had on his relations with the barons. Did other factors do even more damage?

John's reign ended in dramatic fashion. In 1215 a group of leading barons rebelled, forcing their king to agree to Magna Carta – a set of rules by which he would govern the country. Peace did not last long and soon the country was once again at war, as the rebel barons fought to remove John and replace him with Prince Louis of France. This event is known as the First Barons' War. Not all of the leading barons turned against John; men like William Marshal remained loyal to the Crown and fought on the royalist side. However, by the time of John's death in 1216, Louis and the rebel barons controlled half the country and there was the problem of who should succeed John. Why had John's reign ended in such a dramatic way?

Visible learning: Using a summary circle to identify and remember key events

We have divided Chapter 7 into three sections:
- 7.1 The barons' rebellion of 1215
- 7.2 Negotiations at Runnymede and the issuing of Magna Carta
- 7.3 The First Barons' War, the invasion of Prince Louis and the problem of the succession.

With so many important events happening in a short space of time, it is important to identify the key turning points and to find a way to remember them in sequence. You can use a summary circle to help you remember the key turning points.

1215–1217: THE KEY EVENTS

As you work through the three sections of Chapter 7 you will decide on the ten most significant events that occurred between 1215 and 1217.

You will then summarise each of these events in a picture and a phrase in a summary circle – using no more than five words per event. You can use the cartoons on pages 93–94 to help you or you can produce your own visual cues.

We have filled in the fourth segment of your summary circle for you. Magna Carta is seen as one of the most important documents in history and it was certainly a key turning point in John's reign. You need to decide on the three key events that led to Magna Carta and the six events that should go after it.

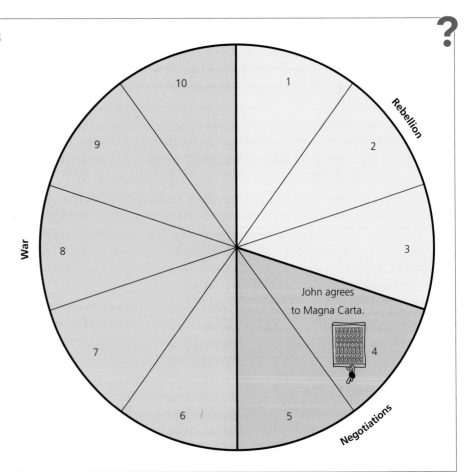

John agrees to Magna Carta.

7.1 The barons' rebellion of 1215

In Chapter 6 you explored the main reasons why John's relationship with the **barons** worsened during his reign (look back at the 4Fs on page 82). These were the longer-term causes of the barons' rebellion in 1215. In this enquiry you will analyse two key questions which focus on the short-term reasons for the rebellion and its immediate consequences.

Key question 1: What happened in the months leading up to the rebellion? Was there a crucial turning point that caused the barons to take up arms against their king?

Key question 2: Why did the rebellion lead to John agreeing to Magna Carta? What were the key events that made John listen to the barons' demands?

THE REBELLION OF 1215

1 Sort the key event cards opposite and on page 94 into a diamond nine that shows the importance of each event. Think carefully about the importance of each event or development in leading to the barons' rebellion and Magna Carta. Use the key questions to help you make your decisions. Explain your decisions using the sentence starters in the diagram or develop your own.

2 Use your diamond nine to decide on the first three events that should be placed in your summary circle on page 92.

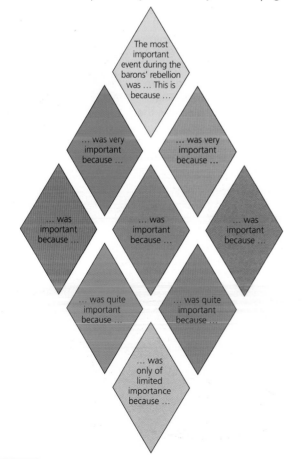

The most important event during the barons' rebellion was … This is because …

… was very important because …

… was very important because …

… was important because …

… was important because …

… was important because …

… was quite important because …

… was quite important because …

… was only of limited importance because …

EVENT 1: LATE 1214

Around the time that John was returning to England from France, some of the leading barons met at Bury St Edmunds. They had with them a copy of Henry I's coronation charter in which Henry had promised to protect the rights and freedoms of people in his kingdom. Each man swore that if John refused to grant the liberties contained within the charter they would go into open rebellion.

EVENT 2: JANUARY 1215

John agreed to meet the barons in London. Here the barons made their demands, centred mainly on Henry I's coronation charter, with some extra provisions added. John refused to accept these demands. However, he agreed to meet the barons again in Northampton in April. John was playing for time.

EVENT 3: EARLY 1215

John started to prepare for war. His castles were restocked and the garrisons strengthened. John began to recruit mercenaries from the **Continent**, adding these to the troops he had brought back with him from Poitou. John seemed to be in a strong position.

EVENT 4: MARCH 1215

John strengthened his position with the Pope when he took the cross at St Paul's cathedral and agreed to go on **crusade**. This guaranteed him the Pope's support in the conflict with the barons.

EVENT 5: APRIL 1215

By April, the barons had lost faith in John and they were no longer prepared for John to merely confirm Henry I's coronation charter. Opposition had grown and so had the demands of the rebels. They now wanted major reforms and intended to force John to make concessions that would be recorded in a new charter. They sent John another set of demands (historians believe that these were probably an early draft of the Articles of the Barons, which became the basis for Magna Carta).

EVENT 6: 5 MAY 1215

When John did not respond to their demands the barons moved into open rebellion. On 5 May they broke their **homage** to John, declared FitzWalter as their leader, and marched on Northampton. The rebel barons lacked siege engines and failed to take Northampton castle, but this was the first open act of warfare.

John offered that the complaints being made against him should be considered by four barons chosen by himself and four chosen by the rebel barons, with the final decision resting with the Pope. With the Pope having the final say, there was little chance of John having to concede too much and the barons rejected John's offer.

EVENT 7: 12 MAY 1215

John ordered that the lands of his enemies should be seized by the sheriffs. By May 1215 only 39 barons had declared themselves as rebels. However, only a similar number openly expressed their support for the King. The majority of barons stood to one side, either not wanting to become involved in the conflict or waiting to see which side gained the advantage.

EVENT 8: 17 MAY 1215

On 17 May a group of barons made their way into the city of London, where they opened the gates to other rebels. They quickly gained control of the capital, although John's forces still held the Tower of London. The citizens of London formed an alliance with the rebels. This was a massive blow for John. The financial resources of the city were now in the hands of the rebels. London's defensive walls meant that it was very hard to attack, and the city was far too large to besiege. After the fall of London, many more supporters joined the rebels. The rebellion had expanded. Young men were attracted to the cause, seeing an opportunity to make a name for themselves.

EVENT 9: THE SUMMER OF 1215

By the summer of 1215, Norfolk and Suffolk were under the control of the rebel barons. A rebel army seized control of the important town of Lincoln, although they failed to take the royal castle in Lincoln, which was bravely defended by Lady Nicola de la Haye. There were major defections from the King's side to the rebels – including two powerful northern barons – Robert de Ros and John de Lacy. The rebels also took control of Northampton, Chester and Carlisle. John was now in a position where he had to listen to the barons' demands. The map shows the key places in the barons' rebellion.

This map shows the towns ▶ which were involved in the events of 1214–1215.

7.2 Runnymede and the motives behind Magna Carta

John needed to buy himself time and, in June, he agreed to meet the barons face to face at Runnymede – a meadow between Windsor and Staines. Here the barons presented him with the Articles of the Barons, their programme of reforms, which would go on to form the basis of Magna Carta. Fifty-six of Magna Carta's sixty-three chapters were based on the demands made in the Articles of the Barons; other chapters were added during the negotiations.

The meeting between the King and the rebel barons went on for a number of days. During the negotiations, the rebel barons arrived in large numbers and Runnymede became an armed camp. John spent most of his time in the safety of Windsor Castle and eventually authorised Magna Carta on 15 June. King John did not sign it; instead Magna Carta was validated by attaching the King's seal.

On 19 June John met the rebel barons in person at Runnymede, where they performed the act of homage to the King. This marked the moment when peace was declared and the terms agreed came into effect. However, it had been also agreed that the barons would continue to hold London until 15 August. The barons wanted to make sure that the charter was acted upon before they left the capital.

Magna Carta was a set of rules about how the King should treat the freemen of England. Peasants were not free men, so Magna Carta did not protect their rights. Knights, merchants and bishops – as well as barons – were freemen. The barons included these other groups in Magna Carta in order to gain more support. Magna Carta was, in many ways, a selfish document in which the barons looked to protect their own interests. It did little for others in society.

However, Magna Carta was clearly a dramatic and important event. We have already included it in the summary circle on page 92. This leaves you free to explore its provisions. Some of the most important provisions from Magna Carta are summarised on page 96, but you should be able to use your knowledge of the historical context to predict what it contained. What would the barons include in the document? What would they want to make sure that the King could no longer do?

◀ Both of these paintings were produced at the end of the Victorian period (c.1900). How do they give very different impressions of what happened at Runnymede?

PREDICTIVE BINGO ?

Use your notes from Chapter 6 to remind yourself of the main reasons for John's worsening relations with the barons. Then play predictive bingo. Divide a piece of paper into nine squares. In each square predict one of the provisions of Magna Carta. Use page 96 to see if you have got a line or a full house!

Stop the king seizing land owned by barons

Magna Carta: The main provisions

Magna Carta had 63 provisions, covering a wide range of issues. The most important are summarised below.

Provision 1 The English Church shall be free. The king must not interfere with the Church.

Provision 2 When a baron inherits land he should not have to pay more than £100 to the king.

Provision 8 No widow shall be forced to marry as long as she wishes to live without a husband.

Provision 9 Neither the king nor his officials will seize any land in payment of a debt, so long as the debtor has moveable goods sufficient to pay the debt.

Provision 12 No scutage or aid (tax) may be raised within the kingdom without its general consent. Taxes from the city of London are to be treated the same.

Provision 20 A freeman shall only be fined in proportion to the seriousness of his offence. The fine should not be so heavy as to deprive him of his livelihood.

Provision 21 Barons should only be fined after a proper trial. The fine should match the crime.

Provisions 28 and 30 No sheriff, constable or other royal official shall take horses, carts, corn or other moveable goods from any man without immediate payment.

Provision 39 No freeman should be arrested, imprisoned and stripped of his possessions without a fair trial.

Provision 40 To no one will the king sell, delay or deny the right to justice.

Provision 45 The king will appoint as constables and sheriffs only men that know the law and are minded to keep it well.

Provision 49 The king will return all hostages given to him by the barons.

Provision 50 The king will remove from their offices certain royal favourites (these are named specifically in the charter).

Provision 51 As soon as peace is restored all foreign mercenaries should leave the country.

Provision 52 Any man who has been deprived or dispossessed of his lands, castles or rights, without the lawful judgment of their peers, will have them returned.

Provision 61 The barons shall choose 25 barons to make certain that the king keeps to this charter. If the king or any of his servants breaks the charter, the 25 barons can take action to make him keep to the charter. This includes seizing the king's castles and lands, but they cannot attack the king himself, his queen or his children.

WHAT CAN MAGNA CARTA TELL US ABOUT JOHN'S REIGN?

1 How many of the provisions actually contained in the Charter did you predict on page 95?

2 Which provisions were you surprised to see? Explain why they surprise you.

3 Which provision do you think would have surprised and angered John the most?

4 Categorise the provisions – which causes are linked to the following issues that annoyed the barons:
   - ☐ Finance – the ways that John tried to raise money to pay for his failed attempt to win back Normandy.
   - ☐ Favourites – the King's choice of officials.
   - ☐ Fairness – a lack of justice and unfair or cruel treatment of the barons.

5 Why was provision 61 included?

6 What does provision 61 tell us about the extent to which the barons trusted John and believed that he would stick to the Charter?

7 Read the information below. Choose one event to go in your summary circle from page 92 after John's authorisation of Magna Carta in June 1215. What was the key event that led to the breakdown of Magna Carta?

Why didn't Magna Carta end John's conflict with the Barons?

Magna Carta is seen as one of the main events in British history and widely regarded as the foundation of the rule of law in England. It is perhaps the most famous document in our history – yet at the time it was a complete failure. Neither side kept to the agreement. The King refused to dismiss his foreign advisers and mercenaries, while the barons refused to leave London. Just over a month later, the King asked the Pope to quash Magna Carta. The Pope issued a papal bull on 24 August, declaring the Charter 'shameful' and 'null and void of all validity forever'. The rebel barons quickly gave up hope of controlling the King and decided to replace John with the son of the King of France, Prince Louis. The result was a civil war, not the peace that Magna Carta was intended to bring.

John never had any real intention of giving up power and being controlled by the council of 25 barons. John used the period of negotiations to strengthen his royal castles and recruit more foreign mercenaries to his army. In October, John redistributed the lands of the rebel barons to his supporters.

THE POSITION IN OCTOBER, 1215

The King
John still had a number of advantages over the rebels:
- He had the money to hire mercenaries and he could afford the engineers and equipment needed for siege warfare.
- He still controlled nearly all the royal castles.
- His army was led by the experienced Earl of Salisbury and Folkes de Breaute.

The rebels
- In contrast, few of the rebel barons had experience of leading armies into battle.
- Only Louis could offer the resources and military strength needed to defeat John.
- This is why the rebel barons took the dramatic step of asking the son of the King of France to replace John as the King of England.

7.3 The First Barons' War, the invasion of Prince Louis and the problem of the succession

By October 1215, war had returned to England. This civil war is known as the First Barons' War (do not worry about the Second Barons' war – this happened a lot later!) You need to select the five key events that shaped the course of the war and determined its outcome. Focus on this enquiry question:

What were the key events of the First Barons' War?

You will use a living graph to help you identify the key turning points in the war as those loyal to the crown (the royalists) fought against the rebel barons and Prince Louis' French army.

Visible learning

Using living graphs to identify turning points

Living graphs are useful in a number of ways:

- They provide a visual **overview** of the story as it unfolds. This helps you keep the 'big picture' in mind.
- They make you think! You need to **evaluate** the importance of each event and how it changed the course of the war. Make sure you annotate your graph to explain your thinking.
- They help you to identify key **turning points**. Look at the graph – you can see that we think the royalists' capture of Rochester was a key turning point as it causes a four point swing in the graph.
- They are useful as a **revision tool** (see page 105) as they contain the really important information on one sheet of paper.
- Your living graph will help you decide on the five key events that will complete the summary circle that you began earlier in this chapter (see page 92).

LIVING GRAPH: PART 1 (1215)

Make a copy of the living graph. As you read pages 99–102 and explore what happened during the First Barons' War, you will plot the events onto the graph in the position you think they should go to show either royalists successes or setbacks – with a short explanation which justifies your decision. You will then be able to use your living graph to decide on the key turning points of the war.

Start the first part of your graph by carrying out the following tasks:

- Look at where we have begun the graph. Think of what you have just read about the position in October 1215 (page 97). Do you agree that we should start at this point on the graph? If you disagree you will need to start your living graph in a different place and explain why.
- Read key events cards 1 and 2 about what happened at Rochester Castle. Do you agree with where we have placed events 1 and 2? You can change each position on the graph but remember to add a short explanation, justifying your decision.
- Use key event card 3 to complete your living graph up to the end of 1215.

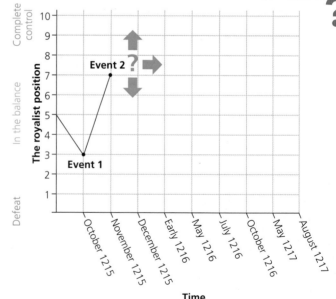

Key

Event 1: October 1215 – rebels gain control of Rochester Castle – would help them defend London

Event 2: November 1215 – royalists gain control of Rochester Castle – major morale boost for John's army

Key events, 1215

The map below shows the main areas of England controlled by the royalists and the rebels between 1215 and 1217.

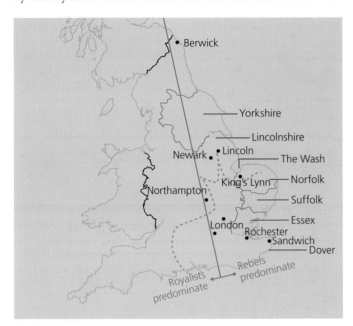

Event 1: October 1215 – The rebels take Rochester Castle

In London, the rebels feared that John might attack them at any moment. In order to delay an attack a group of rebel knights led by William d'Albini took control of Rochester Castle. This castle was in an important position as it stood on the road from Dover to London and would help defend London from attack. John was fully aware of the importance of Rochester Castle and he headed straight for it with a large army.

▼ Rochester Castle.

Event 2: November 1215 – The rebels surrender Rochester

Rochester Castle was made from stone with high walls that were 12 feet thick. The rebels defending the castle hoped to resist John's attack long enough for reinforcements to come from France. However, d'Albini only had 95 knights and 45 soldiers to defend the castle. John's troops quickly captured the town of Rochester and he must have hoped that the size of his army would intimidate the rebels and lead to a quick surrender of the castle.

John set up his siege machines (petraries) and they pounded the walls of the castle with large stones. At the same time he used miners to dig their way under the walls of the castle. John's army was well fed as his men were able to roam the countryside and get food. In contrast, the garrison defending the castle was soon running out of supplies. For six weeks the rebels came under a constant bombardment from the large siege engines and fire from crossbowmen and archers. They must have been physically and mentally exhausted.

Despite being so significantly outnumbered, the rebels continued to defend the castle bravely. Even when miners brought down a large section of the outer curtain wall and John's men advanced, the rebels retreated, still fighting, to the great tower. By now they were so short of food that the rebel knights even had to eat their own horses. Their resistance ended when John ordered 40 slaughtered fat pigs to be sent to Rochester. The pig-fat was used to create a fire strong enough to burn through the mine shaft John's men had dug beneath the great tower. It came crashing down and on 30 November the rebel garrison surrendered.

Event 3: December 1215 – French soldiers start to arrive

In December the first group of French forces landed and made their way to London. Louis promised to arrive with his main force in the new year. The French brought experienced, professional soldiers. They also brought money, supplies and siege equipment.

DECISION TIME

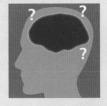

John now faced a crucial decision. Look at John's options at the end of 1215. What would you have done? How would you have built on the success at Rochester?

■ Option 1: Remain at Rochester for the winter and enjoy the victory.
■ Option 2: Attack London as quickly as possible.
■ Option 3: Attack the lands of the rebel barons in East Anglia and the north of England.

Key events, 1216

John now had the opportunity to build on his success and advance on London. Instead he set out on a destructive expedition across the country. John spilt his army into two. One part (under the command of William of Salisbury) remained in the south keeping the rebels pinned down in London. The other part of the army, led by John, marched north with the hope of crushing resistance throughout the rest of the country. This was an opportunity for the King to show his power over the country, collect revenues to fund his army and to do economic damage to the estates held by the rebel barons.

> **LIVING GRAPH: PART 2 (1216)** ?
>
> Use key event cards 4–8 to continue your living graph from page 98 up to the end of 1216. Remember to explain the positions you choose on the graph.

Event 4: Early 1216 – John's campaign in the north

John's campaign in the north of England was very successful. John's reputation had been enhanced by what happened at Rochester. Hearing of the King's approach, many castles held by the rebels were abandoned as their defenders fled to safety. Few barons and knights were willing to hold their castles against him. John's troops reached as far north as Berwick before returning southwards in the spring.

John had gained significant control of the north of England. However, the rebels lived to fight another day. Many retreated into Scotland knowing that John could only stay in the north for a limited time. When John returned south, they seized the opportunity to attack again. John's campaign also lost him a lot of support among his own people because his army acted in a brutal and ruthless way. They even plundered churches and cathedrals, taking money from them in order to pay the troops. The fact that a significant part of his army was made up by foreign mercenaries made it even worse.

Some historians have seen John's decision to advance north as a missed opportunity for him to win the war. They argue that John should have advanced on London before the French started to arrive. The rebellion would have collapsed had London been captured. Instead, John took the safe option and set out on a campaign that unleashed devastation across his own kingdom.

Event 5: May 1216 – Louis arrives

Louis landed in Kent with a large French force in May. John had attempted to blockade Calais and prevent Louis' ships from sailing. However, his fleet was broken up by a large storm and Louis was able to set sail. John could have attacked Louis as he landed his men and resources, but he decided against meeting the French forces in a major battle. Instead, John retreated and the French landed unopposed.

Louis took control of most of Kent and then headed for London, where, on arrival, he was given a tremendous reception. By the summer of 1216, many of John's leading supporters deserted him – even 17 of John's household knights joined the rebels – people were clearly calculating that John was finished!

Event 6: The summer of 1216 – Louis takes control

By the middle of July, Louis and the rebel barons had successfully taken control of Essex, Norfolk and Suffolk. Further north, they took control of Yorkshire and Lincolnshire (but not Lincoln Castle). With two thirds of the barons supporting him, Louis must have been confident of victory. He moved his siege engines to Dover, where he hoped to capture the castle that his father, Philip II, had called 'the key to England'. Dover Castle dominated the south coast and stood in the way of the French being able to safely get troops into England. As the garrison guarding Dover bravely held out, John set out on an expedition, aiming to draw the enemy away from their siege of Dover. John headed towards East Anglia, making his way through enemy territory and burning the houses and crops of rebel barons.

◀ Dover Castle.

Event 7: October 1216 – John's death and the problem of the succession

By the end of September, John was at Lincoln where he broke up the rebels' siege of the castle. He then headed south to King's Lynn. On 12 October, part of his baggage train was lost when it was sucked into the sands as John attempted a short cut across the Wash before the tide had fully gone out. By 15 October John was desperately sick with dysentery. John died in Newark, during the night of 18 October, as a great storm howled around the town.

John's death created a succession problem as his son, Henry, was just nine years old. No child had been crowned king in England for nearly 240 years. This raised the question of who should govern the country on behalf of a child king. The succession of a child to the throne in medieval Europe often led to political unrest as leading barons and members of the royal court saw an opportunity to extend their power and influence. A child king needed a protector who could command respect and maintain royal authority.

The situation in England towards the end of 1216 was particularly precarious because the country was in the middle of a brutal civil war and Louis and the rebel barons controlled almost half the country. To make matters worse, London was controlled by the rebels and there was little money left in the royal treasury to finance the war. The only advantage the royalists had was their system of royal castles.

Event 8: William Marshal becomes Protector

Just before he died, John had placed the kingdom and his son, Henry, under the protection of William Marshal. It was William who took responsibility for organising the King's funeral and the coronation of John's son as king. On 11 November, the leading barons who had remained loyal to John formally named William Marshal as protector of the nine-year-old King Henry III, and regent of the kingdom. Marshal decided to take the young King and his court to Bristol, where they reissued Magna Carta. The aim was to tempt rebel barons back into the young King's camp – by agreeing to the thing that they had been fighting for. Louis did not respond by issuing a charter of his own. In 1217, under William Marshal's energetic and experienced leadership, the royalists began to fight back.

Which three words best sum up why William was such a good choice for Protector?

WHY WAS WILLIAM MARSHAL A GOOD CHOICE FOR PROTECTOR?

- Son of a minor nobleman, he trained to be a knight in Normandy.
- Developed his military skills at tournaments for knights where he proved himself to be strong and brave. After one tournament William's helmet had been knocked so out of shape that he could not get it off until he found a blacksmith who hammered it back into shape – with William's head still inside it!
- Served Henry II loyally. When Henry's sons rebelled, William fought for Henry, knocking Richard off his horse during one battle.
- Richard recognised William's loyalty and military skill, rewarding him at the start of his reign.
- One of the richest men in the kingdom. He had gained control of land in England, Wales, Ireland and Normandy through his marriage to the daughter of the Earl of Pembroke.
- Supported John's claim to the throne and served with him in Normandy (1200–03) but fell out with John after William did homage to Philip II in order to keep his lands in Normandy. John later attacked William's land in Ireland.
- By 1212 William was back in favour with John and stayed loyal to him when many leading barons turned against John during the civil war.

▲ Effigy of William Marshal, First Earl of Pembroke, from his tomb in Temple Church, London.

Key events, 1217

At the start of 1217 Louis decided to return to France. This was a risky move but he needed more men and money to provide resources. With Louis absent, some rebel barons decided to swap sides and join the royalist camp. One of their reasons was frustration at having to compete with Louis' French soldiers for rewards and patronage. During March and April the royalist army, under the command of William Marshal, started to make some gains along the south coast. Meanwhile the English navy made it difficult for Louis to bring in reinforcements and supplies from France.

Event 9: May 1217 – The Battle of Lincoln

On returning to England, Louis decided to divide his army into two. He remained at Dover while another section of his army moved northwards. By May they had reached Lincoln, where they planned to attack the royal castle. William Marshal saw an opportunity to take advantage of Louis' decision to split his army. William formed a large army and marched on Lincoln. They arrived on 20 May, by which time the rebel barons and Louis' men controlled the city of Lincoln and were attacking the castle.

The royalist army, with the 70-year-old William Marshal leading the charge, launched their main assault on the northern gate, which the rebels and French rushed to defend. Meanwhile, a smaller group of royalist troops entered the city by the western gate and made their way to the castle on foot. Royalist crossbowmen made their way to the ramparts of the castle and soon the French and rebel soldiers found themselves coming under a hail of arrows. The rebel army was under attack on two fronts as royalist troops attacking the northern gate were able to break into the city. Eventually, after six hours of vicious hand-to-hand fighting, the French retreated. Those French soldiers who survived were attacked by local people with swords and clubs as they made their way through towns on their way back to London. The Battle of Lincoln was a tremendous success for the royalists. Nearly all the leading barons who had fought for Louis were taken prisoner, along with an estimated 380 knights. In addition, after the battle, over 150 barons and knights abandoned Louis and switched to the royalist's side.

Event 10: August 1217 – The Battle of Sandwich

Louis' hopes of winning the war now rested on new troops arriving from France, where his wife (Blanche of Castile) had managed to put together a large force. The army may have been large enough to help Louis conquer the whole kingdom. It would certainly have helped Louis remain in England for a long period of time and lengthen the war. William Marshal, aware of the threat, ordered his admiral (Philip d'Albini) to watch the seas carefully and stop a French arrival. Meanwhile, William gathered together a large army at the port of Sandwich.

On 24 August, the French fleet set sail for the mouth of the Thames. The English fleet went to meet them. The fleets were roughly equal in terms of fighting vessels but the English were more experienced in naval warfare, especially in the English Channel. The iron-tipped English galleys rammed into the French ships, sinking many of them immediately. The leader of the French fleet (Eustace the Monk) was taken prisoner, after which the remainder of his fleet fled back to France. Eustace offered 10,000 marks for his freedom, but his head was cut off, stuck on a spear and paraded through the streets of Canterbury. The loss to Louis in terms of men and resources was fatal – he now decided to seek peace and on 12 September formal peace terms were agreed. Louis gave up his claims to the English throne but made sure he got the best terms for his English followers. It was agreed that everyone was to recover the lands that they held at the start of the war.

LIVING GRAPH: PART 3 (1217)

Use key event cards 9 and 10 to complete your living graph from page 93 up to the end of 1217. Remember to explain the positions you choose on the graph.

COMPLETING YOUR SUMMARY CIRCLE

1 Use your living graph to decide on the remaining five events for your summary circle from page 92. You have ten events to choose from, so make sure you identify the key turning points in the war and weigh the importance of each event.

2 Complete your circle by summarising each event that you have chosen in a picture and a phrase – using no more than five words per event. You will need to produce your own visual cues.

How far did William Marshal's leadership save England from a French invasion?

Did you include William Marshal becoming Protector in your summary circle? Some historians have argued that John's death and the change of leader was the key turning point that saved England from a successful French invasion. You can test this argument by using a factors map.

THE ROLE OF WILLIAM MARSHAL ?

The diagram below is called a factors map. It shows you the key reasons why Louis' invasion was unsuccessful. The lines between the factors show you some of the links between them.

1 Write at least one sentence explaining each link. The best way to do this is to draw your own version of the factors map on a piece of large (A3) paper and write your explanations onto your map.

2 Can you think of other links? Add these to your diagram and explain the link.

3 The factors map should help you decide which factors were most important. The most important usually has the most links to other factors. Does your factors map suggest that William Marshal's leadership was a crucial factor in Louis' failure to become King of England?

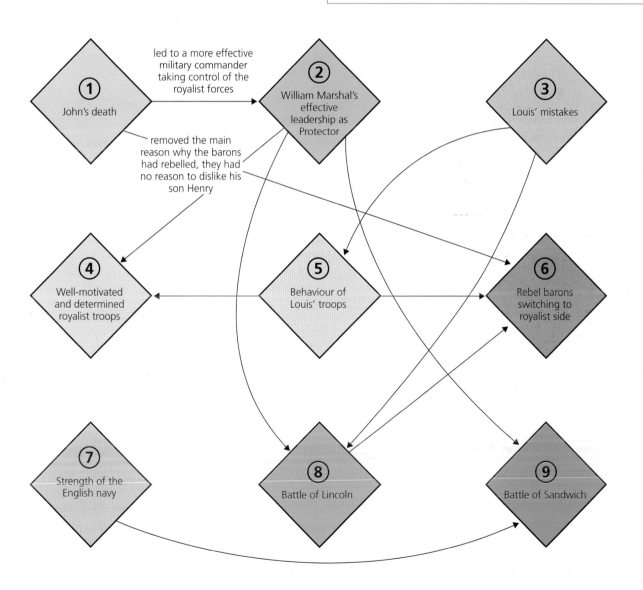

led to a more effective military commander taking control of the royalist forces

removed the main reason why the barons had rebelled, they had no reason to dislike his son Henry

1 John's death

2 William Marshal's effective leadership as Protector

3 Louis' mistakes

4 Well-motivated and determined royalist troops

5 Behaviour of Louis' troops

6 Rebel barons switching to royalist side

7 Strength of the English navy

8 Battle of Lincoln

9 Battle of Sandwich

How has the way that John's reign ended affected his reputation?

The condition that John left England in when he died in 1216 has added to the criticism he has faced from many modern historians. The evidence seems damning.

THE CONDITION OF ENGLAND BY 1216

- Many of barons had rebelled against the Crown – nearly two thirds supported the claim of a foreign prince to the throne.
- John had not been able to resist a foreign invasion.
- Prince Louis of France and the rebel barons controlled half his kingdom, including the capital city.
- England's borders with Wales and Scotland were far from secure.
- Little money was left in the royal treasury.

ENGLAND IN 1216

1 Look at the bullet points in the box above. How far do you think John was to blame for each of these circumstances? Where would you stand on the continuum line below? You can use evidence from Chapters 6 and 7 to support your argument.

totally to blame	majorly to blame	mainly to blame	partly to blame	not to blame at all

2 Read the information below. Can you think of any other factors in John's defence?

Practice questions

1 Describe two key features of Magna Carta.
2 Explain why there was a dispute between John and the Pope.
3 Explain why Magna Carta did not end John's conflict with the barons.
4 'John's failure to recapture his lands in France did the most damage to his relationship with his barons.' How far do you agree? Explain your answer.
5 'William Marshal's leadership was the main reason the French invasion of England failed.' How far do you agree? Explain your answer.

How far did John really leave England in a hopeless situation?

Critics of John have argued that it was only his death that saved the country – had John lived, Louis would have seized control of the whole country and 1066 would not have been the last 'conquest' of England that we remember today. John's death changed everything, taking away the main focus of the baron's anger. His son, Henry, was only nine years of age and was untainted by his father's actions.

However, it could be argued that John's death was not the only significant factor behind Louis' defeat. John did make two decisions that helped to save England. His decision to name William Marshal as his son's Protector was a wise move. William was experienced, respected and a skilled military commander. His decision to reissue Magna Carta in 1216 and allow the lands of rebel barons to be restored if they supported Henry was a clever political move. In doing so, he paved the way for reconciliation and attracted rebel barons back to the royalist side. William also acted decisively at key moments in the war – for example, recognising an opportunity to attack the rebels at Lincoln, and the need to stop the French fleet at Sandwich.

John has also been credited for the way he built up the English navy. When John lost his lands in France it made England far more vulnerable to invasion. A navy became a crucial part of England's defences. To John's credit, he responded to this need. By 1205 he had built a fleet of 46 galleys positioned in 15 different ports from King's Lynn in Norfolk to the south coast. During the rest of his reign the fleet continued to grow in size. Between 1209 and 1212 20 new ships were built. The importance of John's planning was shown in 1217 at Sandwich. England emerged from John's reign as a major naval power.

7.4 Visible learning: revise and remember

Why are summary circles, diamond nines, living graphs and factors maps useful?

They all help you think more clearly and at a higher level. This improves your explanations because you can write more clearly about the complexity of what happened in the past. All of these strategies can be applied to other topics and will help you revise more effectively.

Prioritising and remembering the key events

The summary circle (page 92) and the diamond nine (page 93) help you prioritise events. This is important because in the exam you will not have time to write about everything that happened during a particular period. The summary circle and diamond nine help you to select what to include in an exam answer.

The summary circle can also help you with revision. Only having the space to write down a key word or a phrase makes you think about what is really important, while the visual cues should help with recall.

> Use a summary circle with six segments to help you remember the causes, key events and consequences of John's dispute with the papacy (see Chapter 6, pages 80-81).

Prioritising factors

The diamond nine can also help you **prioritise factors** and develop a clear line of argument. It is a lot easier to write a good answer that is focused on the question if you have a clear line of argument in your head before you begin to write. Diamond nines help you decide which factors were the most important before you begin your answer. Successful students spend time thinking about their approach to the question before they start to write.

> Use a diamond nine to prioritise the factors in the diagram on page 103 that help to explain why Louis was unsuccessful in his attempt to invade England.

Explaining the links between the most important factors

The factors map (page 103) helps you understand that factors are often interlinked. It also helps you to decide which factors were most important. The most important usually has the most links to other factors.

> Produce a factors map that explains John's worsening relations with the barons between 1207 and 1214 (see page 80).

Identifying key turning points

Timelines help you to remember the sequence of events and to build up a 'big picture' of a period or development. However, adding another axis and producing a living graph (page 98) can help you identify trends, patterns and key turning points.

> Produce a living graph that helps you build a big picture of the whole of John's reign (Chapters 5–7, pages 64–104). Use it to identify the key long-term and short-term events that led to John's downfall.

8.1 Reaching a judgement on the kings' reputations

In Chapter 1 we introduced you to the controversy that surrounds the reputations of Richard and John. The medieval chroniclers tended to see Richard as a heroic, successful king and John as an incompetent failure. However, for many years historians have argued about the reputation each monarch deserves. Richard remains a controversial figure, provoking disagreement and debate among historians. Although John's reign ended in failure – he lost most of his Empire and his **barons** rebelled against him – historians disagree about the reasons why.

Now that you have completed your study of Richard and John you are in a strong position to reach your own judgement on the big question that we asked at the start of this book.

The activity below will help you reach your own judgements on the reigns of Richard and John. It will also provide a good test of how much you can remember about the key events and key issues of the period. The cards on pages 107–108 cover many of the events and issues that you need to know about for the exam. The page numbers on each card show you where to go to in the book if you need to refresh your memory.

ASSESSING RICHARD AND JOHN

Step 1: Sort the event cards on pages 107–108 into chronological order and place them on your own copy of the timeline below.

Step 2: Think carefully about the impact each event should have on Richard's or John's reputation. How far did it enhance (use the positive scale) or damage (use the negative scale) their reputation? Move the event card up or down depending on your opinion. Make sure you can justify the position.

Step 3: When you have placed all your event cards on the graph you should be able to reach a verdict on the key questions surrounding Richard's and John's reign. Use the key events cards as evidence to support your answers. You can also add key event cards of your own.

Step 4: Compare your judgements with those of other students in your class. What are the main areas of disagreement? Debate these issues, making sure you support your arguments by referring to the key events.

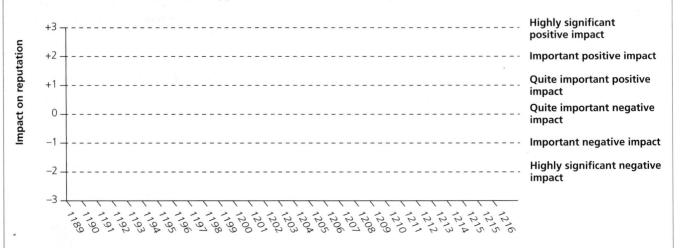

Assessing Richard

How Richard raised funds for the Third Crusade

(page 39)

The conquest of Cyprus

(page 51)

The siege of Acre

(page 52)

Richard's attack on Philip at Vendome

(page 66)

The Treaty of Jaffa

(page 57)

The treatment of prisoners at Acre

(page 53)

Richard's alliance with Philip II and their attack on Henry II

(page 4)

Richard's death at Chalus-Chabrul

(page 67)

Richard's actions on becoming king – his use of patronage

(page 36)

The construction of Château Gaillard

(page 66)

The Battle of Arsuf

(page 55)

The two advances on Jerusalem

(page 56)

Richard's return from the Holy Land

(pages 60–62)

The defence of Verneuil

(page 66)

How money was raised for Richard's ransom

(page 61)

Key questions

1 How far do you agree that Richard managed the barons and used patronage effectively?
2 How far do you agree that England was governed effectively in Richard's absence?
3 How far do you agree that Richard's financial policies caused major problems in England?
4 How far do you agree that the Third Crusade was unsuccessful?
5 How far do you agree that Richard's war against Philip II was successful?
6 Look at the image of Richard on this page. You first saw it on page 2 in the introductory chapter. How far do you now think that this is a fair representation of Richard?

Richard was a military genius, a skilled diplomat and a clever politician. Despite facing dangerous and strong opponents, Richard strengthened the position of the Christians in the Holy Land and defeated Philip II. Richard set up a strong system of government and this meant that England was governed effectively while he was out of the country.

Richard neglected England and wasted its resources. He was obsessed with fighting wars and did not care about governing England. Richard was not a skilled politician and he left behind major problems for his brother. His military record should not be exaggerated – on the Third Crusade he made mistakes and failed to recapture Jerusalem.

Assessing John

The death of Matilda de Briouze and her son

(page 85)

The fall of Château Gaillard

(page 74)

The rescue of Eleanor of Aquitaine at Mirebeau

(page 71)

The murder of Arthur

(page 72)

John's excommunication from the Church

(page 81)

The Thirteenth (a tax on moveables and income)

(page 84)

Louis takes control of much of Eastern England

(page 100)

Negotiations at Runnymede

(page 95)

The Interdict

(page 80)

The rebel barons take control of London

(page 94)

John's alliance with Philip II and the plot against Richard

(page 60)

The siege of Rochester

(page 99)

The Treaty of Goulet

(page 35)

John's reconciliation with Pope Innocent III

(page 81)

The Battle of Bouvines

(page 90)

The breaking of Magna Carta

(page 97)

John was simply unlucky – Richard had left him in a weak position and he had little support. John was an intelligent, hard-working monarch who faced an almost impossible task to hold onto his empire and keep his barons happy. He faced so many problems, yet came close to success – John deserves our sympathy.

John was untrustworthy, aggressive and cruel. He was useless at managing the barons and a very poor soldier. John was an incompetent king who created his own problems.

Key questions

1. How far do you agree that John was to blame for the loss of Normandy?
2. How far do you agree that John's financial policies were too harsh?
3. How far do you agree that John was to blame for the dispute with the Papacy?
4. How far was John to blame for the worsening relations with the barons?
5. How far was John to blame for the failure to win back his lands in France in 1214?
6. How far was John to blame for the success of Louis and the rebel barons during the First Barons' War?
7. Look at the image of John on this page. You first saw it on page 3 in the introductory chapter. How far do you now think that this is a fair representation of John?

Reaching a final judgement

Historians do not always agree with each other. They love to debate and argue. Historians build on the work of earlier historians, deepening and sometimes challenging those earlier interpretations. Interpretations can change for a number of reasons:

- Historians use different sources or choose to use different parts of the same source.
- Historians read the written sources (chronicles, letters, legal documents, poems, songs) in different ways.
- Historians might have different beliefs or come from different backgrounds.

This is your chance to build on the work of historians and reach a final judgement on Richard and John.

HISTORIANS ON RICHARD AND JOHN

Look at the interpretations of Richard and John below and on page 110.

1 Where would the historian place Richard or John on the continuum line below?
2 Identify the main points each historian is making.
3 What events could be used to support each of these points?
4 How far do you agree with the overall interpretation?

| Deserves a very positive reputation | Deserves a positive reputation | Deserves a mixed reputation | Deserves a negative reputation | Deserves a very negative reputation |

Interpretations of Richard

Interpretation 1: Extracts from *King John*, 2nd edn. by W.L. Warren, published in 1997

Richard was generally disliked in his own day. He was an ungracious boor … obsessed with fighting. He was lionhearted but soulless. Warcraft was his speciality and everything else was sacrificed to indulging it. Richard was anxious to be off on the exciting adventure of a crusade … Everything was sacrificed to raise money for it, even good government. His father's officials, who had been loyal to the last, were made to pay heavily to gain the King's goodwill. Everything was for sale – privileges, lordships, earldoms, sheriffdoms, castles, towns.

Richard was no judge of men and an ignorant and irresponsible monarch. Richard had a military flair that John lacked, especially when it came to leading from the front. Richard was indifferent to the business of government and administration.

Men respected his skill and his strategic sense, but there was little for which to love him. He might seem heroic at a distance but those who lived under his rule received the news of his death with relief.

vs.

Interpretation 2: Extracts from *Richard I* by John Gillingham, published in 1999

Thanks to the efforts of Saladin, Leopold of Austria and Philip II, few rulers can have faced greater difficulties than Richard. No earlier or later king took on a challenge remotely comparable with the task of taking a fleet to the eastern end of the Mediterranean and there facing, even facing down, an adversary as formidable as the great Saladin. The conquest of Cyprus and the recovery of the coastal cities of Palestine brought substantial and lasting gain. Had he headed straight for Jerusalem … it could not have been held for long.

[In 1194] Richard left the kingdom in the care of one of the most outstanding ministers in English history, Hubert Walter … Hubert Walter was a resounding success. No king had a better servant.

Richard taxed more heavily than his father. Complaints against the level of taxation were coupled with an acceptance that the money was properly spent on a just war by a ruler who, unlike his father, was admired by his own subjects.

The Empire collapsed in 1203–04 because John's shortcomings as a ruler enabled King Philip to take advantage. In 1198–99 Richard was winning the war against Philip. This was in part because he was a highly competent ruler, unusually effective across the whole range of a king's business, administrative, diplomatic and political as well as military.

Interpretations of John

Interpretation 3: Extracts from an article by Graham E. Seel published in *History Today*, February 2012

There had never been a king who devoted himself so keenly to the job of ruling. John's government was vibrant and forward-looking. A close study of the record evidence calls into question the stereotype of a wicked John, to be replaced by an image of a monarch possessed of terrific energy.

His reign coincided with what most historians agree were two peculiarly resilient and clever adversaries: Philip Augustus of France and Pope Innocent III (r. 1198–1216).

The loss of European possessions was more the result of structural deficiencies than the inadequacies of John, it was naturally disposed to fracture. Moreover John's inheritance was made yet more problematic because it seems likely that England was financially exhausted in 1199.

John's refusal to accept the papal nominee, Stephen Langton, as Archbishop of Canterbury fits well with the fact that each of his predecessors had at some point experienced tensions with the Church.

[Magna Carta] as a peace settlement was always destined to be short-lived … Acceptance would have rendered John a phantom king. No monarch of the time could have accepted Magna Carta.

If John's forces had won at the great set piece battle at Bouvines in 1214 (and they almost did), then it seems as though there would have been no Magna Carta and no civil war.

vs.

Interpretation 4: Extracts from a post published on the *History Today* website in 2015 by Marc Morris

By the time of his death in 1216, and for centuries thereafter, John was regarded as the worst king ever to have sat on England's throne, a reputation that was well deserved. John was treacherous, tyrannous, cowardly and cruel. He betrayed his elder brother, Richard the Lionheart, by trying to usurp the throne while Richard was on crusade.

He extorted more money from his English subjects than any king since the Norman Conquest. He inherited a vast dominion on the Continent, including Normandy, Anjou and Aquitaine, but lost almost all of it and failed to win any of it back. He took prisoners and hostages, several of whom he starved to death.

In the end John's subjects rose up in arms against him and demanded reform, forcing the King to commit to Magna Carta. When he rejected the charter a few weeks later the result was chaos and civil war. The English barons offered his crown to the son of the king of France, who invaded and occupied half of the country, including London. John died with his kingdom in flames and his reputation deservedly in tatters … Reputations rise and fall, but King John's deserves to remain at the very bottom.

YOUR FINAL JUDGEMENT ON RICHARD AND JOHN **?**

1 The images to the right show the covers of recent books published by the historians who produced Interpretations 3 and 4. You can tell by the title what each author thinks of King John. What title would you choose for a book on King John?

2 What title would you choose for a book on King Richard?

3 How would you sum up the reigns of Richard and John? Write a post for a website in which you state what reputation each king deserves. Your post should be no longer than 300 words.

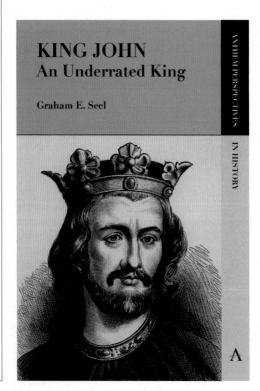

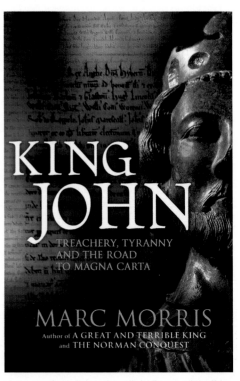

8.2 Visible learning: Effective revision

Step 1: Create the big picture

The first step when it comes to revision is to create a big picture of the course. You can use the graph you have just created for revision. It is useful to have an overview of the key events and issues. However, in the exam you will also be tested on your knowledge and understanding of society at the time. What was the big picture of English society between 1189 and 1216?

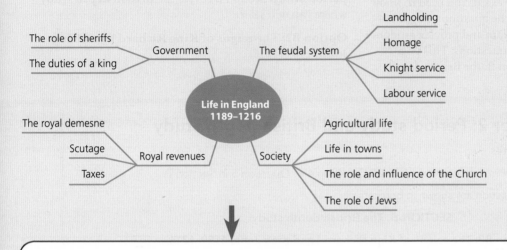

Review your notes from Chapters 2 and 3. Aim to reduce your notes to one 'big picture' using a mind map. Add details to the mind map opposite

Step 2: Remember the important details

When you have got a good overview of the 'big picture', you need to make sure you can remember the key details of specific events. Making revision cards can help. On one side of the revision card write a summary of the key event. On the other side write questions that will test your knowledge of the key event. You can use the revision cards to get someone to test you at home or at school.

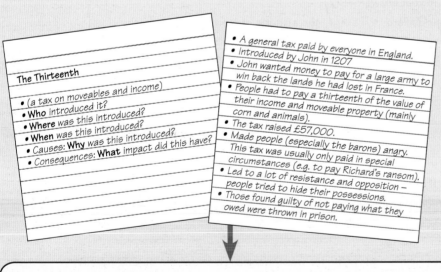

Produce revision cards on the key events in the Third Crusade (see Chapter 4), the fight for Normandy (see Chapter 5), the barons' rebellion of 1215, the First Barons War and the invasion of Prince Louis (see Chapter 7).

Step 3: Test – Reflect – Review – Retest

You need to regularly test your knowledge of the key events. Use the results of the test to plan the next stage of your revision programme. You can use a traffic light system to help you reflect on what you feel confident with and what you need to go back over.

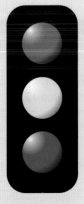

Red – Struggling to remember this – revise again in detail and retest

Orange – Remembered most of this – go back over and retest

Green – Remembered all the key points

Writing better history

Introducing the exam

Simply knowing a lot of content is not enough to achieve a good grade in your GCSE History exam. You need to know how to write effective answers to the questions. Pages 114–122 give you an insight into the exam and provide guidance on how to approach the different questions. This page introduces the structure of Section B (the British depth study) of your Paper 2 exam. The guidance opposite on page 113 helps you approach your exam with confidence.

Paper 2 is divided into two sections. Section A covers the **period study**. Section B covers the **British depth study** where you will select:

Option B2: The reigns of King Richard I and King John, 1189–1216.

Paper 2: Period study and British depth study

(1) **Time**: 1 hour 45 minutes

Answer all questions from Section A and EITHER Question 4 or Question 5 in Section B.

(2) The marks for each question are shown in brackets.

SECTION B: The British depth study

Option B2: The reigns of King Richard I and King John, 1189–1216

(3) Answer Question 5(a), 5(b) and EITHER 5(c)(i) or 5 (c)(ii).

(4) 5 **(a)** Describe **two** features of the role of sheriffs in the years 1189–1216. (4 marks)

Feature 1:

Feature 2:

(5) **(b)** Explain why John had lost Normandy by 1204. (12 marks)

(6)
> You may use the following in your answer:
> - the loss of Château Gaillard
> - the attitude of Normandy's barons.
>
> You **must** also use information of your own.

(7) Answer EITHER (c)(i) OR (c)(ii)

EITHER

(8) **(c)(i)** 'Serious financial difficulties were the main consequence of England's involvement in fighting overseas in the years 1189–1204.' How far do you agree? Explain your answer. (16 marks)

> You may use the following in your answer:
> - war against Philip II of France
> - Richard I's ransom.
>
> You **must** also use information of your own.

OR

(c)(ii) 'King John's failure to regain his lands in France was the main reason for the barons' rebellion of May–June 1215.' How far do you agree? Explain your answer. (16 marks)

> You may use the following in your answer:
> - taxes
> - the Battle of Bouvines.
>
> You **must** also use information of your own.

Planning for success

1 TIMING

It is important to time yourself carefully. One hour and 45 minutes sounds a long time but it goes very quickly! Section A (period study) and Section B (depth study) are worth the same amount of marks. You should aim to spend the same amount of time on each section. For both the period study and the depth study, it is important to have a time plan and to stick to it.

Look at the plan below. You could use this plan or develop your own and check it with your teacher. We have broken down the depth study into two 25 minute blocks of time. This is because some students spend too long on Questions 5(a) and 5(b). They then rush Question 5(c). However, the final question is worth the same amount of marks as 5(a) and 5(b) put together.

Section A (period study) Question 1, 2 and 3: approx. 50 minutes

Section B (depth study on the reigns of King Richard I and King John) Question 5: approx. 50 minutes

Question 5 (a) and 5(b): approx. 25 minutes

EITHER Question 5 (c) (i) OR and 5(c) (ii): approx. 25 minutes

Checking answers: 5 minutes

2 SPEND TIME DE-CODING QUESTIONS

The marks for each question are shown in brackets. This gives you an idea of how much you need to write, as does the space for your answer on the exam paper. However, do not panic if you do not fill all the space. There will probably be more space than you need and the quality of your answer is more important than how much you write. The most important thing is to keep focused on the question. If you include information that is not relevant to the question you will not gain any marks, no matter how much you write!

Read each question carefully before you to start to answer it. Use the advice on de-coding questions on page 114 to make sure you focus on the question.

3 FOLLOW INSTRUCTIONS CAREFULLY

Read the instructions very carefully. Some students miss questions they need to answer while others waste time answering more questions than they need. Remember to answer Question 5(a) **and** 5(b). You then need to choose between **EITHER** Question 5(c)(i) OR 5(c)(ii).

4 THE 'DESCRIBE' QUESTION

The first question on Section B asks you to describe two features of an aspect of the period you have studied. Headings on the exam paper help you write about each feature separately. Advice on how to gain high marks on this type of question is on page 115.

5 THE 'EXPLAIN' QUESTION

The second question tests your ability to write effective explanations. You may be asked to explain why an event or development took place. Pages 116–117 help you write a good answer to this type of question.

6 USING THE STIMULUS MATERIAL

When you attempt Question 5(b) and either Question 5(c) (i) or (c)(ii) you will have bullet points as stimulus material to help plan your answer. You do not have to include them but try to use them to get you thinking and to support your arguments. You must bring in your own knowledge too. If you only use the stimulus material you will not gain high marks for your answer.

7 THINK CAREFULLY ABOUT WHICH QUESTION YOU CHOOSE

When it comes to the choice of final question, do not rush your decision. Think carefully about which question you will do best on. Plan your answer – it is worth 16 marks, half the available marks for Section B of the exam paper.

8 THE 'JUDGEMENT' QUESTION

This question carries the most marks and requires a longer answer that needs careful planning. You will be provided with a statement and you will have to reach a judgement as to how far you agree with that statement. Pages 118–119 provide advice on answering this style of question.

CHECKING THE QUALITY OF YOUR WRITING

Make sure you leave five minutes at the end of the exam to check your answers. If you are short of time check your answer to the final question first as it carries the most marks. Page 119 provides advice on what to focus on. Remember that the accuracy of your spelling, punctuation and grammar is important in all questions as it affects the clarity of your answer.

De-coding exam questions

The examiners are not trying to catch you out: they are giving you a chance to show what you know – and what you can do with what you know. However, you must stick to the question on the exam paper. Staying focused on the question is crucial. Including information that is not relevant or misreading a question and writing about the wrong topic wastes time and gains you no marks.

To stay focused on the question you will need to practise how to 'de-code' questions. This is particularly important for Section B of the exam paper. Follow these **five steps to success**:

Step 1 Read the question a couple of times. Then look at **how many marks** the question is worth. This tells you how much you are expected to write. Do not spend too long on questions only worth a few marks. Remember it is worth planning the 12 and 16 mark questions.

Step 2 Identify the **conceptual focus** of the question. What is the key concept that the question focuses on? Is it asking you to look at:

- the **significance** of a discovery or individual
- **causation** – the reasons why an event or development happened
- **consequence** – the results of an event or development
- **similarities and differences** – between the key features of different periods
- **change** – the extent of change or continuity, progress or stagnation during a period?

Step 3 Spot the **question type**. Are you being asked to:

- **describe** – the key features of a period
- **explain** – similarities between periods or why something happened
- reach a **judgement** – as to how far you agree with a particular statement.

Each question type requires a different approach. Look for key words or phrases that help you work out which approach is needed. The phrase 'How far do you agree?' means you need to weigh the evidence for and against a statement before reaching a balanced judgement. 'Explain why' means that you need to explore a range of reasons why an event happened.

Step 4 Identify the **content focus**. What is the area of content or topic the examiner wants you to focus on?

Step 5 Look carefully at the **date boundaries** of the question. What time period should you cover in your answer? Stick to this carefully or you will waste time writing about events that are not relevant to the question.

Look at the exam question below. At first glance it could appear that this question is about how King John failed to regain his land in France in 1214. This shows the danger of not de-coding a question carefully. If you simply describe how or why John failed to defeat Philip and regain his land in France you will not be focusing on the question. If you explain how his defeat at the hands of Philip made the barons more likely to rebel, you would gain a few more marks but you are still not focusing on the actual question.

The conceptual focus is causation – you need to reach a judgement on whether John's failure to regain his lands in France was the main cause of the baron's rebellion.

The content focus is more than just John's failure to regain his lands in France. It is exploring a wider theme – the reasons for the barons' rebellion.

5 (c) (ii) 'King John's failure to regain his lands in France was the main reason for the barons' rebellion of May–June 1215.' How far do you agree? Explain your answer. (16)

There are 16 marks available – this means the question requires an extended answer. It is definitely worth planning your answer to this question!

The phrase 'How far do you agree' means that this question requires you to reach a judgement about the statement in quotation marks. This means analysing the impact of John's defeat in 1214. It also means weighing the importance of this cause of the barons' rebellion against other important causes (such as the way he treated the barons and his financial policies).

The dates provided for the barons' rebellion are important. The question is asking you to focus on the reasons why the barons rebelled in May–June 1215. If you include references to why the barons went to war with John after Magna Carta was sealed you will waste time and not pick up any additional marks.

REMEMBER

It is worth spending time de-coding questions carefully in the exam. It helps you focus on the question and stops you wasting time including information that is not relevant.

Further practice

Look at the other questions in Section B of the exam paper on page 112.

Break each question down into the five steps and check you have de-coded the question effectively.

Describing key features of a period

'Describe' questions only carry 4 marks so it is important to get to the point quickly so you do not waste precious time needed for questions that carry 12 or 16 marks.

Look at the question below.

> Describe **two** features of the role of sheriffs in the years 1189–1216. **(4 marks)**
>
> Feature 1: _____
>
> Feature 2: _____

Tip 1: Stay relevant to the question

One major problem with 'Describe' questions is that students write too much! They include details that are not relevant to the question. Make sure you stick to the question – describe two key features of what sheriffs did during the reigns of Richard and John.

You do not need to:

- include more than two features (extra features will gain you no more marks)
- evaluate and reach a judgement as to whether sheriffs played a more important role in governing England than individuals who did other jobs for the king
- go beyond the date boundaries and describe how the role of the sheriff changed in the late Middle Ages.

If you write too much you could run out of time later in the exam when you are answering questions that are worth a lot more marks and need longer answers.

Tip 2: Keep it short and simple

You can get 2 marks by simply identifying two features of the role of sheriffs.

For each feature you identify add a sentence that adds further detail and develops your answer.

Look at the example below. Then practise your technique by tackling the examples in the exam practice box.

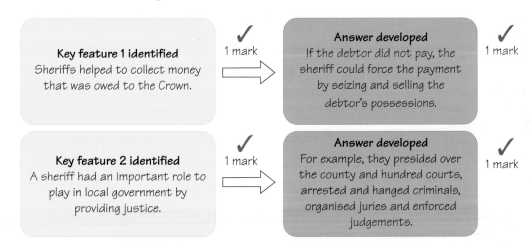

Key feature 1 identified
Sheriffs helped to collect money that was owed to the Crown.

✓ 1 mark

Answer developed
If the debtor did not pay, the sheriff could force the payment by seizing and selling the debtor's possessions.

✓ 1 mark

Key feature 2 identified
A sheriff had an important role to play in local government by providing justice.

✓ 1 mark

Answer developed
For example, they presided over the county and hundred courts, arrested and hanged criminals, organised juries and enforced judgements.

✓ 1 mark

Practice questions

1 Describe two features of knight service in the years 1189–1216.
2 Describe two features of labour service in the years 1189–1216.
3 Describe two features of peasant life in the years 1189–1216.
4 Describe two features of life in towns in the years 1189–1216.
5 Describe two features of the role of the Church in the years 1189–1216.

Further 'describe' practice questions can be found on pages 16, 28, 41, 77 and 104.

REMEMBER

Stay focused and keep it short and simple. Four sentences are enough for four marks.

Writing effective explanations: Tackling '12 mark' Explain questions

Look at the question below.

> **5(b)** Explain why John had lost Normandy by 1204. (12 marks)
>
> You may use the following in your answer:
> - the loss of Château Gaillard
> - the attitude of Normandy's barons
>
> You **must** also use information of your own.

The conceptual focus is on causation (explaining **why** an event took place). The question is worth 12 marks. The examiner will expect you to give a range of reasons **why** John had lost Normandy by 1204.

It is important to spend time planning this question during your exam. Follow the steps below to help you plan effectively and produce a good answer.

Step 1: Get focused on the question

Make sure you de-code the question carefully. Note that the content focus is on the loss of Normandy and the date boundary is 'by 1204'. Do not go into John's attempts to defeat Philip and win back Normandy ten years later.

Step 2: Identify a range of factors

Try to cover more than one cause. If your mind goes blank the stimulus bullet points can also help you. For example, in the question above, 'the loss of Château Gaillard' should make you remember to analyse military reasons for the loss of Normandy. Remember – you are expected to go beyond the bullet points and bring in your own knowledge – so do not be put off if a factor that you want to write about is not covered by the bullet points provided.

Step 3: Organise your answer using paragraphs

Do not worry about a long introduction. One or two sentences is more than enough and you can use words from the question. Look at the example below. Note how the student has built a short introduction into the first paragraph which focuses on the role played by military factors.

In 1199 John inherited a vast Empire, but by 1204 he had lost control of nearly all of his land overseas, including the wealthy and strategically important duchy of Normandy. One important reason for the loss of Normandy was that John made poor military decisions. For example, his failure to defend Château Gaillard meant that …

Aim to start a new paragraph each time you move onto a new factor that caused change. Signpost your argument at the start of the paragraph. For example, you could start your next paragraph like this:

John also faced a skilled, well-resourced and determined opponent. Philip II …'

Step 4: Do not 'say' that a factor was important – PROVE it was

Remember that a list of reasons for John's loss of Normandy will not get you a high level mark. You need to PROVE your case for each factor. This means developing your explanation by adding supporting information and specific examples (killer evidence).

This is where your work on connectives will come in useful. Look again at the advice on page 58 and remember to tie what you know to the question by using connectives such as 'this meant that', 'this led to' and 'this resulted in'. For example, you may want to build on the opening to your first paragraph by proving that John's failure to defend Château Gaillard was a key turning point.

John's failure to defend Château Gaillard meant that *that Philip could now launch an attack on Rouen, the capital of Normandy. Within three months Philip had control of the whole of Normandy. It also* resulted in *the collapse of resistance to Philip II. The castle symbolised control of Normandy and the Norman barons lost confidence in John after Château Gaillard surrendered.*

Step 5: End your answer with a thoughtful conclusion

Keep your conclusion short. A good conclusion makes the overall argument clear – it is not a detailed summary of everything you have already written! Make it clear which factor played the most important role. You may want to show how it links to other factors.

Advice	Model
Start by showing that you are aware that a range of factors played a role.	Philip II was a skilled military commander who had the resources needed to make it difficult for John to keep control of Normandy.
Make it clear which factor you think played the most important role.	However, it was never inevitable that John would lose complete control of the Duchy so quickly. The key reason this happened was because John made a number of poor military decisions.
Support your argument with your key reason why you have come to this conclusion.	John's half-hearted and unsuccessful attempt to stop the French army taking control of Château Gaillard and his failure to confront the French King in battle opened the door for Philip II to seize control of Normandy.

Practice questions

You can find further 'explain' practice questions on pages 26, 28, 41, 48, 58, 75, 77, 91 and 104.

REMEMBER

Do not try to cover too many reasons for an event. Select which causes you can make the strongest argument for. Remember in the exam you will have approximately 15 minutes to answer this question.

Making judgements – tackling the 16-mark question

The last question on the exam paper carries the most marks and requires a carefully planned, detailed answer. You will be provided with a statement in quotation marks and be asked to reach a judgement about **how far you agree** with it. The phrase 'how far' is important as it is unlikely that you will totally agree or disagree with the statement. The examiner will be looking for you to show that you can weigh the evidence for and against the statement.

Look at the example below.

> **(c)(i)** 'Serious financial difficulties were the main consequence of England's involvement in fighting overseas in the years 1189–1204.' How far do you agree? Explain your answer. (16 marks)
>
> You may use the following in your answer:
> - war against Philip II of France
> - Richard I's ransom.
>
> **You must** also use information of your own.

Follow the same steps that you would for an explain question (see page 116).

Step 1: Focus

The content focus is important – you have to reach a judgement on the main consequence of England's involvement in fighting overseas in the years 1189–1204. The conceptual focus is on consequences. Focus on the phrase 'main consequence' in the question – do you think financial problems were 'the main consequence' of England's involvement in wars between 1189 and 1204?

- Think of how Richard's absence from England gave John a chance to cause problems in England and Philip the opportunity to invade his lands in France.
- Think of how Richard's victories over Philip gained him the respect of people in England, particularly the barons, while John's losses to Philip did the reverse and led to a loss of confidence in John.
- Were there more important consequences?

Step 2: Identify

The 16-mark questions require you to reach a judgement on a statement. In order to do this effectively you need to identify **clear criteria** for reaching that judgement. Just like you need to cover a range of factors in 'explain' questions, you need to **cover a range of criteria** in 'judgement' questions.

Possible criteria for reaching a judgement:

- You could evaluate how wide-ranging the consequences were. Did the fighting overseas have mainly financial/economic consequences or were there important political consequences as well?
- You could also analyse how many people were affected by the event. Did the severe financial problems caused by the constant fighting overseas between 1189 and 1204 create problems for a large number of people or only a few?

Step 3: Organise

The simplest way to plan for judgement-style questions is to think in terms of 'for' and 'against' paragraphs:

- Paragraph 1 – Evidence to **support** the statement. For example, show how fighting overseas forced Richard and John to raise taxes and extend the ways that the Crown raised money. This led to increased financial pressure being placed on the barons – which in turn created resentment.
- Paragraph 2 – Evidence to **counter** the statement. Show how the decisions taken to join the crusade and fight wars against the King of France had important political consequences – particularly growing dissatisfaction and resentment among the barons.
- Paragraph 3 – Your final conclusion – weigh the evidence – how far do you agree with the statement?

Step 4: Prove

Remember to tie what you know to the question. Do not include information and think that it will speak for itself. Some students think that simply dropping in examples to the right paragraphs is enough. The following statement from a student could be further developed and gain more marks.

> Another important consequence of England fighting overseas in the period 1189–1204 was that Richard I was captured on his journey back to England from fighting in the Holy Land.

This does not **prove** that Richard I's capture had important consequences. The student needs to go on to explain **how** his capture meant that a huge sum of money had to be paid in return for his release from prison. This affected many people in England as taxes were increased to raise funds to pay the ransom.

Step 5: Conclude

Your conclusion is a crucial part of your answer. You have been asked to reach a judgement on a statement. You need to clearly state how far you agree with it and your reason why. It would be easy to sit on the fence and avoid reaching a final conclusion. But sitting on the fence is a dangerous position. Your answer collapses and you lose marks.

Instead of sitting on the fence, you need to be confident and reach an overall judgement. Imagine that you have placed the evidence on a set of scales. How far do they tip in favour of the statement or against it?

You can then move on in your conclusion to explain your judgement. Do not repeat everything you have already written. Think of the scales – what are the heaviest pieces of evidence on each side? Build these into your conclusion in the following way:

Advice

Model

Advice	Model
JUDGEMENT – Start with your judgement – try to incorporate words from the question into this sentence.	To a large extent, I agree that significant financial problems were the main consequence of England's involvement in fighting overseas in the years 1189–1204.
COUNTER – Show that you are aware that there is some evidence to counter this and give the best example.	The loss of Normandy resulted in serious political problems for John as it led to the barons losing confidence in his ability to launch major military campaigns.
SUPPORT – Explain why, overall, you have reached the judgement you have. Give your key reason or reasons why.	However, the financial strains caused by funding Richard's crusade, paying his ransom and the wars against Philip II were even more significant. Taxes were raised to levels that had never been seen before and royal government was extended in order to find new ways to raise funds.

Practice questions

You can find further 'judgement' practice questions on pages 28, 41, 77, 91 and 104.

REMEMBER

Two important warnings.

Firstly, leave enough time to **check your answer** carefully for spelling, punctuation and grammar.

- Is your spelling and punctuation accurate?
- Does your work make sense? Are your arguments clear?
- Have you used a wide range of historical terms?

Secondly, **beware of iceberg questions**!

Spot the part of the question that lurks beneath the water. Remember what we said about de-coding judgement questions like the one below (see page 77). You need to weigh the importance of the cause in the question against the importance of other causes (such as John's financial policies, his choice of advisers and the way he treated the barons).

(c)(ii) 'King John's failure to regain his lands in France was the main reason for the barons' rebellion of May–June 1215.' How far do you agree? Explain your answer. (16 marks)

What are the key ingredients of effective writing in GCSE history?

The language you use to express your ideas is very important. One of the ways to get better at history is to be more precise with your use of language. For example rather than simply saying that you **agree** or **disagree** with a statement you can use language that shows whether you agree to **a large extent** or only **to some extent**. Look at the different shades of argument below and experiment with using some of the phrases. Use them when you are debating or discussing in class.

Thinking carefully about the language you use

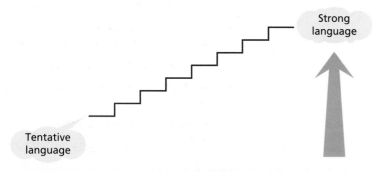

Varying your language to show how far you agree with a statement:	Varying your language to show how important a factor/cause is:
I totally/entirely/completely/absolutely agree with …	… was by far the most important reason why …
I substantially/fundamentally/strongly agree with …	The key/crucial/essential factor was …
I agree to a large extent with …	… was the main cause of …
I mainly/mostly agree with …	The most influential cause was …
I agree to some extent with …	… played a significant/important/major role in …
I partially/partly agree with …	… was of some importance in …
I only agree with … to a limited/slight extent.	
Varying your language to show the significance or importance of an individual, discovery, event or development:	**Varying your language to show the extent of change:**
… made the most important/significant contribution to …	… was revolutionised in …
… had a crucial/major/highly significant impact on …	… totally changed during …
… had an important/influential impact on …	… was transformed during …
… was of some importance/significance	… there was fundamental change in …
… only made a limited/partial/slight/minimal contribution to …	The period saw significant/important progress in …
	… saw some changes in …
	… saw some progress in …
	… saw limited/slight/minimal progress in …

Helpful phrases and sentence starters		
When you want to explore the other side of an argument: On the other hand … However … Alternatively, it could be argued that …	**When you want to highlight similarities:** In the same way … Similarly … This is similar to the way that … Likewise …	**When you want to make an additional point to support an argument:** Also … Additionally … In addition … Moreover … Furthermore …
When you want to link points or show that one thing led to another: Therefore … Due to … Consequently … One consequence of this was … This caused … This led to … This resulted in … This meant that …	**When you want to give examples to support a point:** For example … For instance … This can be seen when … This is clearly shown by … This is supported by … This is proven by …	**When you want to show that an individual, event or discovery was important:** … was a crucial turning point in … … acted as an important catalyst for … Without this event/development/discovery … would not have happened. This had an immediate impact on … In the short term this transformed/revolutionised … In the long term this had a lasting impact on …

You can use the **progression grid** below to get an idea of what getting better at history looks like. This is designed to give you a general idea of what you need to do to produce good answers in the exam. It focuses on the four key things in the white squares on the bingo card on page 122.

	Question focus	Organisation	Line of argument	Supporting information
High level ↑	The answer is consistently focused on the question.	The answer is structured very carefully and explanations are coherent throughout.	The line of argument is very clear and convincing. It flows throughout the answer.	Supporting information has been precisely selected and shows wide-ranging knowledge and understanding.
	The answer is mainly focused on the question.	The answer is well organised but some parts of the answer lack coherence.	The line of argument is clear, convincing and generally maintained through the answer.	Support information is accurate and relevant and shows good knowledge and understanding.
	The answer has weak or limited links to the question.	Some statements are developed and there is some attempt to organise the material.	The line of argument is partly convincing but not maintained through the answer.	Supporting information is mainly accurate and relevant and shows some knowledge and understanding.
	The answer has no real links to the question.	The answer lacks organisation.	The line of argument is unclear or missing.	Supporting information is limited or not relevant.

Self-assessing and peer assessing your work

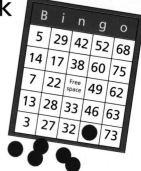

It is important that you check your own work before you hand it to your teacher to be marked. Sometimes you may be asked to assess the work of someone else in your class. In both cases you need to know what you are looking for. What are the key ingredients of great writing in history?

You can use the **bingo card** as a checklist – get competitive and try and show that you have covered all the squares and got a full house of ingredients!

The answer starts with a **clear focus on the question** (there is no long introduction). Key words from the question are used during the answer. For longer answers, each paragraph is linked to the question.	Statements and arguments are fully developed and explained – showing good knowledge and understanding. Arguments are **well supported** by accurate, relevant and well selected evidence.	**Connectives** are used to help prove arguments and show significance/impact. Look for phrases like: *this led to …* *this resulted in …* *this meant that …*
There is a **clear line of argument** at the start of each paragraph – think of it as a signpost for what follows. The rest of the paragraph supports this argument. The line of argument flows throughout the answer building up to a clear conclusion.	Paragraphs have been used to provide a **clear structure**. Each paragraph starts with a different cause/factor (12-mark explain questions) or a different theme/criteria (16-mark judgement questions	The answers shows **wide ranging** knowledge and understanding. It considers a range of factors/causes (explain questions) or explores the evidence for **and** against a statement ('judgement' questions)
The language used helps to construct very precise arguments – showing how important the writer thinks a cause/factor, event or individual is. A good range of specialist **historical vocabulary** has been used.	There is a **clear conclusion**. For explain questions factors/causes are prioritised or linked. For judgement questions there is a focus on 'how far' the writer agrees with the statement.	The answer has been **carefully checked** for spelling, punctuation and grammar. The meaning is always clear throughout the answer.

Glossary

Agents   Men who served the king and help to rule a specified area

Anti-Semitism   Hostility, prejudice or discrimination against Jews

Arbitrary power   Decisions taken by an individual based on their own wishes, as opposed to being based on law or agreed principles

Barons   A man who holds a barony (land) from the king

Bishoprics   The Church district controlled by a bishop, often containing many churches

Byzantine Empire   An empire of the eastern Mediterranean region, dating from AD 395 when the Roman Empire was partitioned into eastern and western portions

Chancellor   The head of the chancery. This was an office that travelled with the king and wrote and sealed the king's charters and letters

Charter   A document that gave people certain rights and privileges

Chroniclers   People who wrote books describing historical events or the life of a nobleman

Continent   One of the world's seven large landmasses. The land held by Richard and John on the Continent refers to land they held outside of England in the Continent of Europe

Crucify   An ancient punishment in which an individual was nailed or bound to a cross

Crusade   Wars between Christian and Muslim armies in the area around Jerusalem (called the Holy Land)

Distaff   A tool used in spinning. It is designed to hold the unspun fibres, keeping them untangled

Duchy   The land controlled by a Duke

Earldoms   The land ruled over by an Earl, often but not always a county

Excommunicate   A punishment that banned an individual from being a member of the Church

Feudal hierarchy   The way in which society was structured in the Middle Ages. This was based on gaining land from those above you in society in return for providing them with military service or labour

Financial impositions   Money paid by individuals as a result of demands forced on them by a king or someone in authority

Flank   The right or left side of a military formation

Forfeiture   The loss of land or property as a punishment for treason or a criminal act

Holy Land   The area around Jerusalem

Homage   The ceremony in which a new tenant swore loyalty to his tenant-in-chief. This ceremony created a bond of loyalty

Indulgence   A declaration by Church authorities that those who say certain prayers or do good deeds will not have to spend so long in Purgatory. A full indulgence meant that a person's soul could pass straight to Heaven, without going through Purgatory

Interdict   A punishment from the Pope that bans certain church services. Under the 1208 Interdict no-one was allowed to attend Mass or bury their deceased relatives in consecrated ground with religious ceremony. Only the baptism of infants and the confessions of the dying were permitted

Justiciar   The king's chief minister; the man who was in charge of the government during the king's absence from the kingdom

Knight service   The agreement by which a tenant promised to provide a number of knights to his lord in return for land. Tenants-in-chief (barons) held their land from the king by knight's service and therefore had to provide knights for the king's army

Labour service   The services owed by an unfree tenant to his lord in return for land. This involved providing agricultural labour to the lord, often on a weekly basis

Landholding   A piece of land owned or rented by an individual or group of individuals

Makkah   Islam's holiest city, the birthplace of the Prophet Muhammad

Ministers   servants of the king who carried out his wishes and commands

Moveables   Moveable property, especially corn and animals

Offices   An important position that helped the king run the country

Overlord   A lord who had power or authority over other lords

Papal bull   A letter or announcement from the Pope

Patronage   The power to control appointments to office or the right to privileges

Peasant   People who worked on the lord's land or for a free tenant. They had no rights and could not leave their manor (village) without their lord's permission

Pogroms   A violent attack, massacre or persecution of a minority group

Principality   Land ruled over by a prince or monarch

Privileges   A special right or advantage, granted to a particular group

Protector   A person who would look after the king and govern the country if the new monarch was too young or unable to rule

Purgatory   People believed that this was the place where the spirits of dead people went to before they were ready to go to Heaven. In Purgatory they would have to suffer for the evil acts they did while alive

Regent   A person appointed to rule a kingdom if the new king was too young to rule

Royal demesne   Land controlled directly by the king, rather than land held from him by a tenant-in-chief

Royal exchequer   The part of the royal government that was responsible for collecting and counting the king's annual revenue

Scutage   Money owed by a tenant-in-chief in place of sending a quota of knights to the king

Seneschal   A member of the royal household in charge of domestic arrangements and the administration of servants

Sheriff   The man that the king put in charge of a county

Shi'ite Muslims   Muslims who believed that Muhammad's successor should come from his family. They believed that Muhammad's proper successor was his son-in-law and cousin Ali ibn Abi Talib

Sunni Muslims   Muslims who believed that after Muhammad's death his successor should be appointed by an election. They believe that Muhammad's father-in-law Abu Bakr, not Ali ibn Abi Talib, was his proper successor

Vassal   A person granted the use of land, in return for homage and usually military service

Index